Reconnecting Youth

Student Workbook

Leona L. Eggert and Liela J. Nicholas

Solution Tree | Press a division of Solution Tree

555 North Morton Street
Bloomington, IN 47404
800.733.6786 (toll free) / 812.336.7700
FAX: 812.336.7790

email: info@solution-tree.com
solution-tree.com

Printed in the United States of America

FSC
www.fsc.org
MIX
Paper from
responsible sources
FSC® C011935

ISBN 978-1-935249-37-5 (Student Workbook)
ISBN 978-1-932127-18-8 (6-Volume Leader's Guide Set)
_____

Illustrator: Barbara Murray Sullivan
Cover Designer: Grannan Graphic Design

Getting Started

Getting Started

A new set of classes, a different schedule. . . . When you think about the weeks ahead, you might feel like you're standing at the bottom of a mountain. You look up and see the mountain top—the end of these classes—but it seems so far away. I'm just getting started, you think. How will I ever make it to the top?

There's good news for you in *Reconnecting Youth.* Just by joining the group, you're already on your way to the top. That's because you're already an expert on one of *Reconnecting Youth's* main subjects: *you.* No one knows better than you do

- what you like and dislike about yourself;

- what makes you angry, sad, or happy;

- where you've been;

- what you're struggling with now; and

- what you want to become in the future.

And that's where *Reconnecting Youth* starts—with you right now.

Reconnecting Youth will show you ways to take control of your life and overcome the obstacles you face. You'll take control of your journey by using the *Reconnecting Youth* strategies that work for you. You can raise your grades. You can improve your drug-use control. You can get along better with your teachers. And you can improve the way you feel about yourself.

Joining the *Reconnecting Youth* group is a step toward a better future. The next step you take is up to you.

RY: An Overview

The purpose of *Reconnecting Youth* is to accomplish the goals listed in the center of this page. Each group member plays a big part in the group's achievement of those goals. Write your name and the names of the group members on the blank lines surrounding the goal circle.

_____   _____

_____   **PROGRAM GOALS**   _____

1. Improve School
Performance
_____   (Grades, Credits,   _____
Attendance, Work)

2. Improve Drug-Use
_____   Control   _____

3. Improve Mood
Management

_____   _____

_____   _____

Guidelines for Our Group to Follow

Think about how you would like our group to function. How should we treat one another? What guidelines do we need to follow in order to develop group trust? What guidelines should we have for confidentiality? What guidelines would be important to you? Write these guidelines below.

◉ _____

◉ _____

◉ _____

◉ _____

◉ _____

Now work with a partner. Look at and discuss each other's lists. Agree on your top five choices, using items from both lists. List those items below. We will then work as one group to develop our group guidelines.

1. _____

2. _____

3. _____

4. _____

5. _____

Our Group Guidelines
for Showing Care and Concern

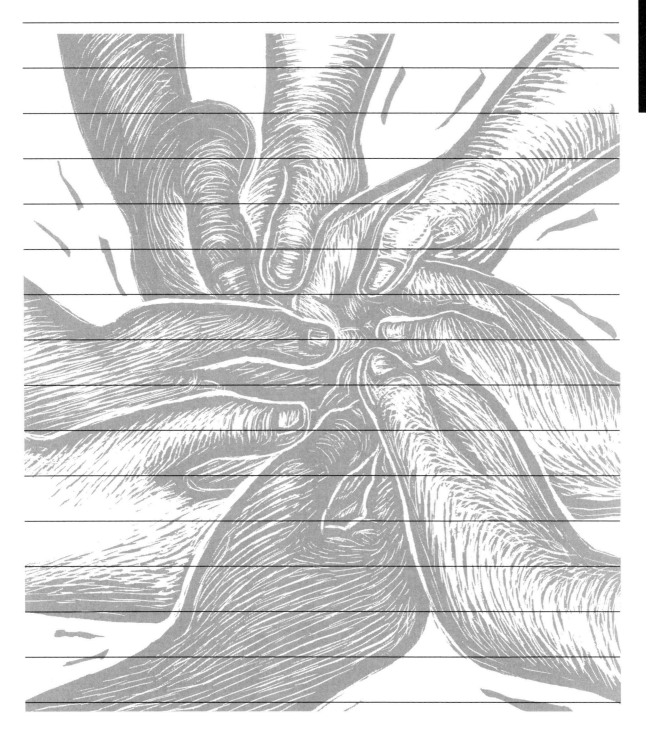

Difficult or Pleasant Issues That Might Come Up in Group

Examples of Difficult or Pleasant Issues

- Broke up with a boyfriend or girlfriend

- Got a good grade on a test or made the team

- _____

- _____

- _____

- _____

- _____

Examples of Hurtful Responses

- That was dumb! No wonder she broke up with you.

- _____

- _____

- _____

Examples of Helpful Responses

- I'm sorry to hear that. Breakups are hard.

- _____

- _____

- _____

Practice Giving Helpful Responses

Briefly describe a situation where a helpful response would be appropriate. Keep it simple. Keep it brief.

_____

_____

_____

Identify two possible hurtful responses to this situation.

⚡ _____

⚡ _____

Identify three possible helpful responses to this situation.

☀ _____

☀ _____

☀ _____

Develop a short role play to practice giving helpful feedback.

Person 1: Briefly describe the situation.

Person 2: Listen and then provide a brief, helpful response that supports Person 1. (Do not try to solve the problem.)

Person 1: Thank Person 2, and say how the helpful response felt.

Switch roles, and do a second role play.

Role Plays
for Showing Care and Concern

Situations Related to School

1. I always fail math and this teacher is awful. I know I'll fail again.

2. I'm hanging out with my friends at lunch, and I'm not going to my afternoon classes. Maybe I should drop those classes.

3. I really dislike my history teacher. She always picks on people. I think I'll quit going to that class.

Situations Related to Drug Use

1. My kid sister is starting to fool around with pot. She's too young to be messing up already.

2. We're all smoking dope at lunch. I think my seventh period teacher knows. He's probably going to bust us.

3. I promised my mother I would quit using all of this stuff, but everyone is doing it. How can I stop when everyone does it?

Situations Related to Mood Management

1. My girlfriend (boyfriend) broke up with me and is now going out with my best friend.

2. My parents were really fighting last night. No one got any sleep. It's really tense at home right now.

3. I don't care how much trouble I get into. I'm going to get even with this teacher.

CONTRACT TO PRACTICE

Showing Care and Concern

1. Choose a person you know who is hurting right now or someone who could probably use some care and concern. This could be a friend, family member, neighbor, or someone else. Write the person's name below.

2. Practice giving a helpful message to this person that shows care and concern. Write your message below.

_____

_____

_____

_____

_____

_____

_____

Be prepared to report back to the group on how this went the next time we meet.

CONTRACT TO PRACTICE

Improving My Attendance

In the next 24 hours, I will improve my attendance by . . .

_____

_____

One predictable barrier that could stop me from doing this is . . .

_____

_____

My barrier tempts me not to improve my attendance by . . .

_____

_____

I respond appropriately when I resist my barrier by . . .

_____

_____

My barrier tempts me again by . . .

_____

_____

I successfully remove the barrier and keep my attendance goal by . . .

_____

_____

Sample School Smarts Checklist

❏ Do you *go to class?*

❏ Do you *do homework outside of class?*

❏ Do you *ask for help?*

❏ Do you *negotiate with teachers?*

❏ Do you *set goals you **can** achieve?*

❏ Do you *ask how you are doing and keep track of your progress?*

❏ Do you *confront your fears . . . of tests . . . of teachers?*

❏ Do you *deal with disappointments and start over?*

❏ Do you *praise yourself for working hard and achieving goals?*

❏ Do you *take care of yourself?*

CONTRACT TO PRACTICE

Keeping My School Smarts Goal

My School Smarts goal is . . .

_____

_____

One predictable barrier that could keep me from meeting my goal is . . .

_____

_____

With your partner, practice successfully overcoming the barrier so you can meet your goal!

A note from your partner praising you for how you overcame the barrier and giving you encouragement to keep your goal.

Make a list of feelings you or your partner have experienced during the last 10 days. Include positive and negative feelings.

Happy   *Lonely*   *Hopeful*

Exhausted   _____   suspicious

          _____

Angry   _____   **Confident**

          _____

Embarrassed   _____   Frightened

          _____

Enraged   _____   Depressed

          _____

Confused   _____   JEALOUS

          _____

bored   _____   *Shy*

Ecstatic   **Guilty**

OVERWHELMED

Reconnecting Youth © 2004 Solution Tree

Identifying Moods

1. Think of various moods you have experienced this past week (for example, happy, sad, frustrated, angry, energetic, bored). Write one mood on each self-stick note.

2.   Next, place your self-stick notes in the boxes below.

    *   **Helpful Moods** help you reach your goals and feel good about yourself. This might include a whole range of emotions.

    *   **Hurtful Moods** make it harder for you to reach your goals and also make you feel bad about yourself. These are moods you would like to manage and control better.

Helpful Moods

Hurtful Moods

Drug-Use and Non-Use Decisions

CONFIDENTIAL

Your Name _____

In the space below, draw a graph of your history of drug use or non-use. Use three different colors of pen or pencil:

Green = Cigarettes ▬ ▬ ▬ ▬ ▬   **Blue** = Alcohol ▬▬▬▬   **Red** = All other substances ▬ ▪ ▬ ▪ ▬ ▪

1. Using the green pencil, place a dot at the age when you first smoked. Place the dot in the space between no use and occasional use.
2. Continue placing dots for your level of smoking cigarettes at ages 13, 14, and so on until your current age. Then connect the dots.
3. Make a large X at each key decision point. These points would be times when you remember making a decision that had an effect on whether or not you smoked and on how much you smoked.
4. Repeat the process for alcohol using a blue pencil and for other substances using a red pencil.

If you do not use drugs, place an X at each point where you **reconsidered** decisions about whether or not to use.

LEVELS OF USE

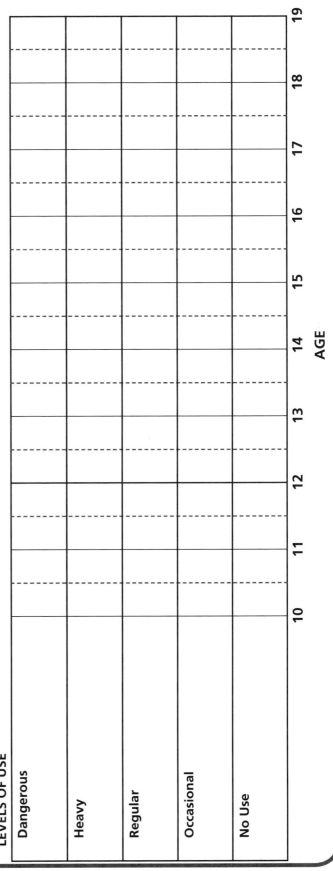

LEVELS OF USE	10	11	12	13	14	15	16	17	18	19
Dangerous										
Heavy										
Regular										
Occasional										
No Use										

AGE

Problems Students Could Experience When Using Drugs

- _____
- _____
- _____
- _____
- _____
- _____

Ways for Students to Decrease Their Drug Use

- _____
- _____
- _____
- _____
- _____
- _____

Sample Attendance Goals

◎ I will attend first period every day for the next 2 weeks.

◎ I will be on time for my class after lunch every day for the next 2 weeks.

◎ I will attend each of my classes at least four times each week for the next 2 weeks.

◎ I will attend all of my classes for the next 2 weeks.

◎ I will have no more than three skips each week for the next 2 weeks.

◎ I will be on time for all of my classes for the next 2 weeks.

◎ I will continue to have perfect attendance in my RY class for the next 2 weeks.

◎ I will meet with my English teacher on Friday and begin attending my English class next Monday.

Attendance Goal Worksheet

Your goal should be

DESIRABLE • SPECIFIC • ACHIEVABLE

My attendance goal for the next 2 weeks is . . .

_____

_____

_____

_____

A predictable barrier will be . . .

_____

_____

My response to the barrier will be . . .

_____

_____

Sample School Achievement Goals

◎ I will *do 1 hour of homework each day for the next 2 weeks.*

◎ I will *begin working on my English book report this weekend, and I will have it ready to turn in by Wednesday when it is due.*

◎ I will *talk to my history teacher after school today to get my homework assignments, and I will spend 30 minutes each day doing these assignments until they are done.*

◎ I will *ask my math teacher to change my desk assignment so I am not sitting with my friends.*

◎ I will *go to the tutoring center each day after school for 30 minutes (except on Fridays) to get help with my assignments.*

◎ I will *take notes during class instead of whispering with my friends.*

School Achievement Goal Worksheet

Your goal should be

DESIRABLE • SPECIFIC • ACHIEVABLE

My school achievement goal for the next 2 weeks is . . .

_____

_____

_____

_____

A predictable barrier will be . . .

_____

_____

My response to the barrier will be . . .

_____

_____

A Note of Support and Encouragement From Your Partner About Your Attendance Goal and Your School Achievement Goal

Sample Mood Management Goals

- I will take my dog for a walk if I start to feel depressed.

- I will take a deep breath and count to 10 when I feel like showing my anger with my parents.

- I will get help from my science teacher when I start to feel discouraged in that class.

- I will call my best friend when I need to talk to someone about being depressed.

- I will ask my English teacher to move my desk assignment away from this person I do not like.

- I will not yell back when my mother yells at me. Instead, I will tell her I need to study, and I will go to my room.

- I will ask my friends to go to a movie this weekend so I do not keep thinking about my ex-boyfriend (or ex-girlfriend).

Mood Management Goal Worksheet

Your goal should be

DESIRABLE • SPECIFIC • ACHIEVABLE

My mood management goal for the next 2 weeks is . . .

_____

_____

_____

_____

A predictable barrier will be . . .

_____

_____

My response to the barrier will be . . .

_____

_____

Sample Drug-Use Control Goals

◎   I will continue to stay drug free.

◎   I will support my friends in RY who are trying to cut down on their drug use while I continue to stay drug free.

◎   I will not use any drugs during the school day at school or away from school.

◎   I will smoke no more than 10 cigarettes a day for the next 2 weeks.

◎   I will hang out with my friends who do not use drugs this weekend. I will not use any drugs this weekend.

◎   I will go straight to first period when I get to school so that I am not tempted to use before class.

Decreasing Use or Maintaining No Use Goal Worksheet

Your goal should be

DESIRABLE • SPECIFIC • ACHIEVABLE

My drug-use control goal for the next 2 weeks is . . .

_____

_____

_____

_____

A predictable barrier will be . . .

_____

_____

My response to the barrier will be . . .

_____

_____

A Note of Support and Encouragement From Your Partner About Your Mood Management Goal and Your Drug-Use Control Goal

 # RY Goals

GETTING STARTED

Name_____   Date_____

➤ **School Attendance**
_____
_____

➤ **School Achievement**
_____
_____

➤ **Mood Management**
_____
_____

➤ **Drug-Use Control**
_____
_____

Monitoring Tools

Weekly Attendance

(WEEKS 1–9)

Week Number	Start Date	Day	Periods 1	2	3	4	5	6	7	Goal for the Week	Actual Number of Periods Missed
		M									
		T									
		W									
		TH									
		F									
		M									
		T									
		W									
		TH									
		F									
		M									
		T									
		W									
		TH									
		F									
		M									
		T									
		W									
		TH									
		F									
		M									
		T									
		W									
		TH									
		F									
		M									
		T									
		W									
		TH									
		F									
		M									
		T									
		W									
		TH									
		F									
		M									
		T									
		W									
		TH									
		F									
		M									
		T									
		W									
		TH									
		F									

Weekly Attendance
(WEEKS 10–18)

Week Number	Start Date	Day Periods	Goal for the Week	Actual Number of Periods Missed

Week Number	Start Date	Day	Periods 1 2 3 4 5 6 7	Goal for the Week	Actual Number of Periods Missed
	_____	M T W TH F			
	_____	M T W TH F			
	_____	M T W TH F			
	_____	M T W TH F			
	_____	M T W TH F			
	_____	M T W TH F			
	_____	M T W TH F			
	_____	M T W TH F			
	_____	M T W TH F			

Reconnecting Youth © 2004 Solution Tree

School Smarts Checklist
(WEEKS 1–4)

YOUR NAME _____

School Smarts Strategies	Week 1							Week 2							Week 3							Week 4						
	S	S	M	T	W	T	F	S	S	M	T	W	T	F	S	S	M	T	W	T	F	S	S	M	T	W	T	F
1.																												
2.																												
3.																												
4.																												
5.																												
6.																												
7.																												
8.																												
9.																												
10.																												
11.																												
12.																												
13.																												
14.																												

School Smarts Checklist
(WEEKS 5–8)

YOUR NAME _____

School Smarts Strategies	Week 5							Week 6							Week 7							Week 8						
	S	S	M	T	W	T	F	S	S	M	T	W	T	F	S	S	M	T	W	T	F	S	S	M	T	W	T	F
1.																												
2.																												
3.																												
4.																												
5.																												
6.																												
7.																												
8.																												
9.																												
10.																												
11.																												
12.																												
13.																												
14.																												

School Smarts Checklist

(WEEKS 9–12)

YOUR NAME_____

School Smarts Strategies	Week 9							Week 10							Week 11							Week 12						
	S	S	M	T	W	T	F	S	S	M	T	W	T	F	S	S	M	T	W	T	F	S	S	M	T	W	T	F
1.																												
2.																												
3.																												
4.																												
5.																												
6.																												
7.																												
8.																												
9.																												
10.																												
11.																												
12.																												
13.																												
14.																												

School Smarts Checklist
(WEEKS 13–16)

YOUR NAME _____

School Smarts Strategies	Week 13							Week 14							Week 15							Week 16						
	S	S	M	T	W	T	F	S	S	M	T	W	T	F	S	S	M	T	W	T	F	S	S	M	T	W	T	F
1.																												
2.																												
3.																												
4.																												
5.																												
6.																												
7.																												
8.																												
9.																												
10.																												
11.																												
12.																												
13.																												
14.																												

MONITORING TOOLS

School Smarts Checklist
(WEEKS 17–20)

YOUR NAME _____

School Smarts Strategies	Week 17							Week 18							Week 19							Week 20						
	S	S	M	T	W	T	F	S	S	M	T	W	T	F	S	S	M	T	W	T	F	S	S	M	T	W	T	F
1.																												
2.																												
3.																												
4.																												
5.																												
6.																												
7.																												
8.																												
9.																												
10.																												
11.																												
12.																												
13.																												
14.																												

Mood Diary
(WEEKS 1–4)

My Daily Mood

Your Name_____   Starting Date_____

Please use the scale below and circle the appropriate number above that day's date. Connect the numbers to see how your mood has changed.

Very Sad   **Very Happy**

| 1 | 2 | 3 | 4 | 5 | 6 | 7 | 8 | 9 | 1 0 |

Sad Example_____   Happy Example_____

10	10	10	10	10	10	10
9	9	9	9	9	9	9
8	8	8	8	8	8	8
7	7	7	7	7	7	7
6	6	6	6	6	6	6
5	5	5	5	5	5	5
4	4	4	4	4	4	4
3	3	3	3	3	3	3
2	2	2	2	2	2	2
1	1	1	1	1	1	1
Sat	Sun	Mon	Tue	Wed	Thur	Fri

10	10	10	10	10	10	10
9	9	9	9	9	9	9
8	8	8	8	8	8	8
7	7	7	7	7	7	7
6	6	6	6	6	6	6
5	5	5	5	5	5	5
4	4	4	4	4	4	4
3	3	3	3	3	3	3
2	2	2	2	2	2	2
1	1	1	1	1	1	1
Sat	Sun	Mon	Tue	Wed	Thur	Fri

10	10	10	10	10	10	10
9	9	9	9	9	9	9
8	8	8	8	8	8	8
7	7	7	7	7	7	7
6	6	6	6	6	6	6
5	5	5	5	5	5	5
4	4	4	4	4	4	4
3	3	3	3	3	3	3
2	2	2	2	2	2	2
1	1	1	1	1	1	1
Sat	Sun	Mon	Tue	Wed	Thur	Fri

10	10	10	10	10	10	10
9	9	9	9	9	9	9
8	8	8	8	8	8	8
7	7	7	7	7	7	7
6	6	6	6	6	6	6
5	5	5	5	5	5	5
4	4	4	4	4	4	4
3	3	3	3	3	3	3
2	2	2	2	2	2	2
1	1	1	1	1	1	1
Sat	Sun	Mon	Tue	Wed	Thur	Fri

Mood Diary
(WEEKS 5–8)

My Daily Mood

Your Name_____ Starting Date_____

Please use the scale below and circle the appropriate number above that day's date. Connect the numbers to see how your mood has changed.

Very Sad   **Very Happy**

| 1 | 2 | 3 | 4 | 5 | 6 | 7 | 8 | 9 | 1 0 |

Sad Example_____ Happy Example_____

10	10	10	10	10	10	10
9	9	9	9	9	9	9
8	8	8	8	8	8	8
7	7	7	7	7	7	7
6	6	6	6	6	6	6
5	5	5	5	5	5	5
4	4	4	4	4	4	4
3	3	3	3	3	3	3
2	2	2	2	2	2	2
1	1	1	1	1	1	1
Sat	Sun	Mon	Tue	Wed	Thur	Fri

10	10	10	10	10	10	10
9	9	9	9	9	9	9
8	8	8	8	8	8	8
7	7	7	7	7	7	7
6	6	6	6	6	6	6
5	5	5	5	5	5	5
4	4	4	4	4	4	4
3	3	3	3	3	3	3
2	2	2	2	2	2	2
1	1	1	1	1	1	1
Sat	Sun	Mon	Tue	Wed	Thur	Fri

10	10	10	10	10	10	10
9	9	9	9	9	9	9
8	8	8	8	8	8	8
7	7	7	7	7	7	7
6	6	6	6	6	6	6
5	5	5	5	5	5	5
4	4	4	4	4	4	4
3	3	3	3	3	3	3
2	2	2	2	2	2	2
1	1	1	1	1	1	1
Sat	Sun	Mon	Tue	Wed	Thur	Fri

10	10	10	10	10	10	10
9	9	9	9	9	9	9
8	8	8	8	8	8	8
7	7	7	7	7	7	7
6	6	6	6	6	6	6
5	5	5	5	5	5	5
4	4	4	4	4	4	4
3	3	3	3	3	3	3
2	2	2	2	2	2	2
1	1	1	1	1	1	1
Sat	Sun	Mon	Tue	Wed	Thur	Fri

Mood Diary
(WEEKS 9–12)

My Daily Mood

Your Name_____   Starting Date_____

Please use the scale below and circle the appropriate number above that day's date. Connect the numbers to see how your mood has changed.

Very Sad   **Very Happy**

1   2   3   4   5   6   7   8   9   1 0

Sad Example_____   Happy Example_____

10	10	10	10	10	10	10
9	9	9	9	9	9	9
8	8	8	8	8	8	8
7	7	7	7	7	7	7
6	6	6	6	6	6	6
5	5	5	5	5	5	5
4	4	4	4	4	4	4
3	3	3	3	3	3	3
2	2	2	2	2	2	2
1	1	1	1	1	1	1
Sat	Sun	Mon	Tue	Wed	Thur	Fri

10	10	10	10	10	10	10
9	9	9	9	9	9	9
8	8	8	8	8	8	8
7	7	7	7	7	7	7
6	6	6	6	6	6	6
5	5	5	5	5	5	5
4	4	4	4	4	4	4
3	3	3	3	3	3	3
2	2	2	2	2	2	2
1	1	1	1	1	1	1
Sat	Sun	Mon	Tue	Wed	Thur	Fri

10	10	10	10	10	10	10
9	9	9	9	9	9	9
8	8	8	8	8	8	8
7	7	7	7	7	7	7
6	6	6	6	6	6	6
5	5	5	5	5	5	5
4	4	4	4	4	4	4
3	3	3	3	3	3	3
2	2	2	2	2	2	2
1	1	1	1	1	1	1
Sat	Sun	Mon	Tue	Wed	Thur	Fri

10	10	10	10	10	10	10
9	9	9	9	9	9	9
8	8	8	8	8	8	8
7	7	7	7	7	7	7
6	6	6	6	6	6	6
5	5	5	5	5	5	5
4	4	4	4	4	4	4
3	3	3	3	3	3	3
2	2	2	2	2	2	2
1	1	1	1	1	1	1
Sat	Sun	Mon	Tue	Wed	Thur	Fri

Mood Diary
(WEEKS 13–16)

My Daily Mood

Your Name_____   Starting Date_____

Please use the scale below and circle the appropriate number above that day's date. Connect the numbers to see how your mood has changed.

Very Sad   **Very Happy**

1   2   3   4   5   6   7   8   9   1 0

Sad Example_____   Happy Example_____

10	10	10	10	10	10	10
9	9	9	9	9	9	9
8	8	8	8	8	8	8
7	7	7	7	7	7	7
6	6	6	6	6	6	6
5	5	5	5	5	5	5
4	4	4	4	4	4	4
3	3	3	3	3	3	3
2	2	2	2	2	2	2
1	1	1	1	1	1	1
Sat	Sun	Mon	Tue	Wed	Thur	Fri

10	10	10	10	10	10	10
9	9	9	9	9	9	9
8	8	8	8	8	8	8
7	7	7	7	7	7	7
6	6	6	6	6	6	6
5	5	5	5	5	5	5
4	4	4	4	4	4	4
3	3	3	3	3	3	3
2	2	2	2	2	2	2
1	1	1	1	1	1	1
Sat	Sun	Mon	Tue	Wed	Thur	Fri

10	10	10	10	10	10	10
9	9	9	9	9	9	9
8	8	8	8	8	8	8
7	7	7	7	7	7	7
6	6	6	6	6	6	6
5	5	5	5	5	5	5
4	4	4	4	4	4	4
3	3	3	3	3	3	3
2	2	2	2	2	2	2
1	1	1	1	1	1	1
Sat	Sun	Mon	Tue	Wed	Thur	Fri

10	10	10	10	10	10	10
9	9	9	9	9	9	9
8	8	8	8	8	8	8
7	7	7	7	7	7	7
6	6	6	6	6	6	6
5	5	5	5	5	5	5
4	4	4	4	4	4	4
3	3	3	3	3	3	3
2	2	2	2	2	2	2
1	1	1	1	1	1	1
Sat	Sun	Mon	Tue	Wed	Thur	Fri

Mood Diary
(WEEKS 17–20)

My Daily Mood

Your Name_____   Starting Date_____

Please use the scale below and circle the appropriate number above that day's date. Connect the numbers to see how your mood has changed.

Very Sad   **Very Happy**

1	2	3	4	5	6	7	8	9	1 0

Sad Example_____   Happy Example_____

10	10	10	10	10	10	10
9	9	9	9	9	9	9
8	8	8	8	8	8	8
7	7	7	7	7	7	7
6	6	6	6	6	6	6
5	5	5	5	5	5	5
4	4	4	4	4	4	4
3	3	3	3	3	3	3
2	2	2	2	2	2	2
1	1	1	1	1	1	1
Sat	Sun	Mon	Tue	Wed	Thur	Fri

10	10	10	10	10	10	10
9	9	9	9	9	9	9
8	8	8	8	8	8	8
7	7	7	7	7	7	7
6	6	6	6	6	6	6
5	5	5	5	5	5	5
4	4	4	4	4	4	4
3	3	3	3	3	3	3
2	2	2	2	2	2	2
1	1	1	1	1	1	1
Sat	Sun	Mon	Tue	Wed	Thur	Fri

10	10	10	10	10	10	10
9	9	9	9	9	9	9
8	8	8	8	8	8	8
7	7	7	7	7	7	7
6	6	6	6	6	6	6
5	5	5	5	5	5	5
4	4	4	4	4	4	4
3	3	3	3	3	3	3
2	2	2	2	2	2	2
1	1	1	1	1	1	1
Sat	Sun	Mon	Tue	Wed	Thur	Fri

10	10	10	10	10	10	10
9	9	9	9	9	9	9
8	8	8	8	8	8	8
7	7	7	7	7	7	7
6	6	6	6	6	6	6
5	5	5	5	5	5	5
4	4	4	4	4	4	4
3	3	3	3	3	3	3
2	2	2	2	2	2	2
1	1	1	1	1	1	1
Sat	Sun	Mon	Tue	Wed	Thur	Fri

Drug-Use Control Diary
(WEEKS 1–2)

DRUG USE AND CONSEQUENCES	WEEK OF _____							WEEK OF _____						
ON THIS DAY ➧	Sat	Sun	Mon	Tue	Wed	Thu	Fri	Sat	Sun	Mon	Tue	Wed	Thu	Fri
	(Circle the appropriate number or range of numbers.)							*(Circle the appropriate number or range of numbers.)*						
1. How many cigarettes did you smoke?	0 1–10 11–20 21–30 31–40	0 1–10 11–20 21–30 31–40	0 1–10 11–20 21–30 31–40	0 1–10 11–20 21–30 31–40	0 1–10 11–20 21–30 31–40	0 1–10 11–20 21–30 31–40	0 1–10 11–20 21–30 31–40	0 1–10 11–20 21–30 31–40	0 1–10 11–20 21–30 31–40	0 1–10 11–20 21–30 31–40	0 1–10 11–20 21–30 31–40	0 1–10 11–20 21–30 31–40	0 1–10 11–20 21–30 31–40	0 1–10 11–20 21–30 31–40
2. How many alcoholic drinks did you have?	0 1–2 3–4 5–6 7–8	0 1–2 3–4 5–6 7–8	0 1–2 3–4 5–6 7–8	0 1–2 3–4 5–6 7–8	0 1–2 3–4 5–6 7–8	0 1–2 3–4 5–6 7–8	0 1–2 3–4 5–6 7–8	0 1–2 3–4 5–6 7–8	0 1–2 3–4 5–6 7–8	0 1–2 3–4 5–6 7–8	0 1–2 3–4 5–6 7–8	0 1–2 3–4 5–6 7–8	0 1–2 3–4 5–6 7–8	0 1–2 3–4 5–6 7–8
3. How many times did you use other drugs?	0 1–2 3–4 5–6 7–8	0 1–2 3–4 5–6 7–8	0 1–2 3–4 5–6 7–8	0 1–2 3–4 5–6 7–8	0 1–2 3–4 5–6 7–8	0 1–2 3–4 5–6 7–8	0 1–2 3–4 5–6 7–8	0 1–2 3–4 5–6 7–8	0 1–2 3–4 5–6 7–8	0 1–2 3–4 5–6 7–8	0 1–2 3–4 5–6 7–8	0 1–2 3–4 5–6 7–8	0 1–2 3–4 5–6 7–8	0 1–2 3–4 5–6 7–8
4. How many times did you use more than you intended?	0 1–2 3–4 5–6 7–8	0 1–2 3–4 5–6 7–8	0 1–2 3–4 5–6 7–8	0 1–2 3–4 5–6 7–8	0 1–2 3–4 5–6 7–8	0 1–2 3–4 5–6 7–8	0 1–2 3–4 5–6 7–8	0 1–2 3–4 5–6 7–8	0 1–2 3–4 5–6 7–8	0 1–2 3–4 5–6 7–8	0 1–2 3–4 5–6 7–8	0 1–2 3–4 5–6 7–8	0 1–2 3–4 5–6 7–8	0 1–2 3–4 5–6 7–8
5. How many times did you feel angry, depressed, or in a bad mood afterwards?	0 1 2 3 4	0 1 2 3 4	0 1 2 3 4	0 1 2 3 4	0 1 2 3 4	0 1 2 3 4	0 1 2 3 4	0 1 2 3 4	0 1 2 3 4	0 1 2 3 4	0 1 2 3 4	0 1 2 3 4	0 1 2 3 4	0 1 2 3 4
6. How many times did your use get you into trouble at school?	0 1 2 3 4	0 1 2 3 4	0 1 2 3 4	0 1 2 3 4	0 1 2 3 4	0 1 2 3 4	0 1 2 3 4	0 1 2 3 4	0 1 2 3 4	0 1 2 3 4	0 1 2 3 4	0 1 2 3 4	0 1 2 3 4	0 1 2 3 4
7. How many times did your use cause problems with family or friends?	0 1 2 3 4	0 1 2 3 4	0 1 2 3 4	0 1 2 3 4	0 1 2 3 4	0 1 2 3 4	0 1 2 3 4	0 1 2 3 4	0 1 2 3 4	0 1 2 3 4	0 1 2 3 4	0 1 2 3 4	0 1 2 3 4	0 1 2 3 4
MY DRUG-USE CONTROL GOAL FOR THE WEEK														
DID I ACHIEVE MY GOAL FOR THE WEEK?	❑ Yes ❑ Almost ❑ About Half ❑ Missed It							❑ Yes ❑ Almost ❑ About Half ❑ Missed It						

Drug-Use Control Diary
(WEEKS 3–4)

DRUG USE AND CONSEQUENCES	WEEK OF _____							WEEK OF _____						
ON THIS DAY ▸	Sat	Sun	Mon	Tue	Wed	Thu	Fri	Sat	Sun	Mon	Tue	Wed	Thu	Fri
	(Circle the appropriate number or range of numbers.)							*(Circle the appropriate number or range of numbers.)*						
1. How many cigarettes did you smoke?	0 1–10 11–20 21–30 31–40	0 1–10 11–20 21–30 31–40	0 1–10 11–20 21–30 31–40	0 1–10 11–20 21–30 31–40	0 1–10 11–20 21–30 31–40	0 1–10 11–20 21–30 31–40	0 1–10 11–20 21–30 31–40	0 1–10 11–20 21–30 31–40	0 1–10 11–20 21–30 31–40	0 1–10 11–20 21–30 31–40	0 1–10 11–20 21–30 31–40	0 1–10 11–20 21–30 31–40	0 1–10 11–20 21–30 31–40	0 1–10 11–20 21–30 31–40
2. How many alcoholic drinks did you have?	0 1–2 3–4 5–6 7–8	0 1–2 3–4 5–6 7–8	0 1–2 3–4 5–6 7–8	0 1–2 3–4 5–6 7–8	0 1–2 3–4 5–6 7–8	0 1–2 3–4 5–6 7–8	0 1–2 3–4 5–6 7–8	0 1–2 3–4 5–6 7–8	0 1–2 3–4 5–6 7–8	0 1–2 3–4 5–6 7–8	0 1–2 3–4 5–6 7–8	0 1–2 3–4 5–6 7–8	0 1–2 3–4 5–6 7–8	0 1–2 3–4 5–6 7–8
3. How many times did you use other drugs?	0 1–2 3–4 5–6 7–8	0 1–2 3–4 5–6 7–8	0 1–2 3–4 5–6 7–8	0 1–2 3–4 5–6 7–8	0 1–2 3–4 5–6 7–8	0 1–2 3–4 5–6 7–8	0 1–2 3–4 5–6 7–8	0 1–2 3–4 5–6 7–8	0 1–2 3–4 5–6 7–8	0 1–2 3–4 5–6 7–8	0 1–2 3–4 5–6 7–8	0 1–2 3–4 5–6 7–8	0 1–2 3–4 5–6 7–8	0 1–2 3–4 5–6 7–8
4. How many times did you use more than you intended?	0 1–2 3–4 5–6 7–8	0 1–2 3–4 5–6 7–8	0 1–2 3–4 5–6 7–8	0 1–2 3–4 5–6 7–8	0 1–2 3–4 5–6 7–8	0 1–2 3–4 5–6 7–8	0 1–2 3–4 5–6 7–8	0 1–2 3–4 5–6 7–8	0 1–2 3–4 5–6 7–8	0 1–2 3–4 5–6 7–8	0 1–2 3–4 5–6 7–8	0 1–2 3–4 5–6 7–8	0 1–2 3–4 5–6 7–8	0 1–2 3–4 5–6 7–8
5. How many times did you feel angry, depressed, or in a bad mood afterwards?	0 1 2 3 4	0 1 2 3 4	0 1 2 3 4	0 1 2 3 4	0 1 2 3 4	0 1 2 3 4	0 1 2 3 4	0 1 2 3 4	0 1 2 3 4	0 1 2 3 4	0 1 2 3 4	0 1 2 3 4	0 1 2 3 4	0 1 2 3 4
6. How many times did your use get you into trouble at school?	0 1 2 3 4	0 1 2 3 4	0 1 2 3 4	0 1 2 3 4	0 1 2 3 4	0 1 2 3 4	0 1 2 3 4	0 1 2 3 4	0 1 2 3 4	0 1 2 3 4	0 1 2 3 4	0 1 2 3 4	0 1 2 3 4	0 1 2 3 4
7. How many times did your use cause problems with family or friends?	0 1 2 3 4	0 1 2 3 4	0 1 2 3 4	0 1 2 3 4	0 1 2 3 4	0 1 2 3 4	0 1 2 3 4	0 1 2 3 4	0 1 2 3 4	0 1 2 3 4	0 1 2 3 4	0 1 2 3 4	0 1 2 3 4	0 1 2 3 4
MY DRUG-USE CONTROL GOAL FOR THE WEEK														
DID I ACHIEVE MY GOAL FOR THE WEEK?	❑ Yes ❑ About Half			❑ Almost ❑ Missed It				❑ Yes ❑ About Half			❑ Almost ❑ Missed It			

Drug-Use Control Diary

(WEEKS 5–6)

MONITORING TOOLS

DRUG USE AND CONSEQUENCES	WEEK OF _____							WEEK OF _____						
ON THIS DAY ▶	**Sat**	**Sun**	**Mon**	**Tue**	**Wed**	**Thu**	**Fri**	**Sat**	**Sun**	**Mon**	**Tue**	**Wed**	**Thu**	**Fri**
	(Circle the appropriate number or range of numbers.)							*(Circle the appropriate number or range of numbers.)*						
1. How many cigarettes did you smoke?	0 1–10 11–20 21–30 31–40	0 1–10 11–20 21–30 31–40	0 1–10 11–20 21–30 31–40	0 1–10 11–20 21–30 31–40	0 1–10 11–20 21–30 31–40	0 1–10 11–20 21–30 31–40	0 1–10 11–20 21–30 31–40	0 1–10 11–20 21–30 31–40	0 1–10 11–20 21–30 31–40	0 1–10 11–20 21–30 31–40	0 1–10 11–20 21–30 31–40	0 1–10 11–20 21–30 31–40	0 1–10 11–20 21–30 31–40	0 1–10 11–20 21–30 31–40
2. How many alcoholic drinks did you have?	0 1–2 3–4 5–6 7–8	0 1–2 3–4 5–6 7–8	0 1–2 3–4 5–6 7–8	0 1–2 3–4 5–6 7–8	0 1–2 3–4 5–6 7–8	0 1–2 3–4 5–6 7–8	0 1–2 3–4 5–6 7–8	0 1–2 3–4 5–6 7–8	0 1–2 3–4 5–6 7–8	0 1–2 3–4 5–6 7–8	0 1–2 3–4 5–6 7–8	0 1–2 3–4 5–6 7–8	0 1–2 3–4 5–6 7–8	0 1–2 3–4 5–6 7–8
3. How many times did you use other drugs?	0 1–2 3–4 5–6 7–8	0 1–2 3–4 5–6 7–8	0 1–2 3–4 5–6 7–8	0 1–2 3–4 5–6 7–8	0 1–2 3–4 5–6 7–8	0 1–2 3–4 5–6 7–8	0 1–2 3–4 5–6 7–8	0 1–2 3–4 5–6 7–8	0 1–2 3–4 5–6 7–8	0 1–2 3–4 5–6 7–8	0 1–2 3–4 5–6 7–8	0 1–2 3–4 5–6 7–8	0 1–2 3–4 5–6 7–8	0 1–2 3–4 5–6 7–8
4. How many times did you use more than you intended?	0 1–2 3–4 5–6 7–8	0 1–2 3–4 5–6 7–8	0 1–2 3–4 5–6 7–8	0 1–2 3–4 5–6 7–8	0 1–2 3–4 5–6 7–8	0 1–2 3–4 5–6 7–8	0 1–2 3–4 5–6 7–8	0 1–2 3–4 5–6 7–8	0 1–2 3–4 5–6 7–8	0 1–2 3–4 5–6 7–8	0 1–2 3–4 5–6 7–8	0 1–2 3–4 5–6 7–8	0 1–2 3–4 5–6 7–8	0 1–2 3–4 5–6 7–8
5. How many times did you feel angry, depressed, or in a bad mood afterwards?	0 1 2 3 4	0 1 2 3 4	0 1 2 3 4	0 1 2 3 4	0 1 2 3 4	0 1 2 3 4	0 1 2 3 4	0 1 2 3 4	0 1 2 3 4	0 1 2 3 4	0 1 2 3 4	0 1 2 3 4	0 1 2 3 4	0 1 2 3 4
6. How many times did your use get you into trouble at school?	0 1 2 3 4	0 1 2 3 4	0 1 2 3 4	0 1 2 3 4	0 1 2 3 4	0 1 2 3 4	0 1 2 3 4	0 1 2 3 4	0 1 2 3 4	0 1 2 3 4	0 1 2 3 4	0 1 2 3 4	0 1 2 3 4	0 1 2 3 4
7. How many times did your use cause problems with family or friends?	0 1 2 3 4	0 1 2 3 4	0 1 2 3 4	0 1 2 3 4	0 1 2 3 4	0 1 2 3 4	0 1 2 3 4	0 1 2 3 4	0 1 2 3 4	0 1 2 3 4	0 1 2 3 4	0 1 2 3 4	0 1 2 3 4	0 1 2 3 4
MY DRUG-USE CONTROL GOAL FOR THE WEEK														
DID I ACHIEVE MY GOAL FOR THE WEEK?	❏ Yes ❏ About Half			❏ Almost ❏ Missed It				❏ Yes ❏ About Half			❏ Almost ❏ Missed It			

Drug-Use Control Diary
(WEEKS 7–8)

DRUG USE AND CONSEQUENCES	WEEK OF _____							WEEK OF _____						
ON THIS DAY ▶	Sat	Sun	Mon	Tue	Wed	Thu	Fri	Sat	Sun	Mon	Tue	Wed	Thu	Fri
	(Circle the appropriate number or range of numbers.)							*(Circle the appropriate number or range of numbers.)*						
1. How many cigarettes did you smoke?	0 1–10 11–20 21–30 31–40	0 1–10 11–20 21–30 31–40	0 1–10 11–20 21–30 31–40	0 1–10 11–20 21–30 31–40	0 1–10 11–20 21–30 31–40	0 1–10 11–20 21–30 31–40	0 1–10 11–20 21–30 31–40	0 1–10 11–20 21–30 31–40	0 1–10 11–20 21–30 31–40	0 1–10 11–20 21–30 31–40	0 1–10 11–20 21–30 31–40	0 1–10 11–20 21–30 31–40	0 1–10 11–20 21–30 31–40	0 1–10 11–20 21–30 31–40
2. How many alcoholic drinks did you have?	0 1–2 3–4 5–6 7–8	0 1–2 3–4 5–6 7–8	0 1–2 3–4 5–6 7–8	0 1–2 3–4 5–6 7–8	0 1–2 3–4 5–6 7–8	0 1–2 3–4 5–6 7–8	0 1–2 3–4 5–6 7–8	0 1–2 3–4 5–6 7–8	0 1–2 3–4 5–6 7–8	0 1–2 3–4 5–6 7–8	0 1–2 3–4 5–6 7–8	0 1–2 3–4 5–6 7–8	0 1–2 3–4 5–6 7–8	0 1–2 3–4 5–6 7–8
3. How many times did you use other drugs?	0 1–2 3–4 5–6 7–8	0 1–2 3–4 5–6 7–8	0 1–2 3–4 5–6 7–8	0 1–2 3–4 5–6 7–8	0 1–2 3–4 5–6 7–8	0 1–2 3–4 5–6 7–8	0 1–2 3–4 5–6 7–8	0 1–2 3–4 5–6 7–8	0 1–2 3–4 5–6 7–8	0 1–2 3–4 5–6 7–8	0 1–2 3–4 5–6 7–8	0 1–2 3–4 5–6 7–8	0 1–2 3–4 5–6 7–8	0 1–2 3–4 5–6 7–8
4. How many times did you use more than you intended?	0 1–2 3–4 5–6 7–8	0 1–2 3–4 5–6 7–8	0 1–2 3–4 5–6 7–8	0 1–2 3–4 5–6 7–8	0 1–2 3–4 5–6 7–8	0 1–2 3–4 5–6 7–8	0 1–2 3–4 5–6 7–8	0 1–2 3–4 5–6 7–8	0 1–2 3–4 5–6 7–8	0 1–2 3–4 5–6 7–8	0 1–2 3–4 5–6 7–8	0 1–2 3–4 5–6 7–8	0 1–2 3–4 5–6 7–8	0 1–2 3–4 5–6 7–8
5. How many times did you feel angry, depressed, or in a bad mood afterwards?	0 1 2 3 4	0 1 2 3 4	0 1 2 3 4	0 1 2 3 4	0 1 2 3 4	0 1 2 3 4	0 1 2 3 4	0 1 2 3 4	0 1 2 3 4	0 1 2 3 4	0 1 2 3 4	0 1 2 3 4	0 1 2 3 4	0 1 2 3 4
6. How many times did your use get you into trouble at school?	0 1 2 3 4	0 1 2 3 4	0 1 2 3 4	0 1 2 3 4	0 1 2 3 4	0 1 2 3 4	0 1 2 3 4	0 1 2 3 4	0 1 2 3 4	0 1 2 3 4	0 1 2 3 4	0 1 2 3 4	0 1 2 3 4	0 1 2 3 4
7. How many times did your use cause problems with family or friends?	0 1 2 3 4	0 1 2 3 4	0 1 2 3 4	0 1 2 3 4	0 1 2 3 4	0 1 2 3 4	0 1 2 3 4	0 1 2 3 4	0 1 2 3 4	0 1 2 3 4	0 1 2 3 4	0 1 2 3 4	0 1 2 3 4	0 1 2 3 4
MY DRUG-USE CONTROL GOAL FOR THE WEEK														
DID I ACHIEVE MY GOAL FOR THE WEEK?	❏ Yes ❏ About Half			❏ Almost ❏ Missed It				❏ Yes ❏ About Half			❏ Almost ❏ Missed It			

Drug-Use Control Diary
(WEEKS 9–10)

DRUG USE AND CONSEQUENCES	WEEK OF _____							WEEK OF _____						
ON THIS DAY ▶	Sat	Sun	Mon	Tue	Wed	Thu	Fri	Sat	Sun	Mon	Tue	Wed	Thu	Fri
	(Circle the appropriate number or range of numbers.)							*(Circle the appropriate number or range of numbers.)*						
1. How many cigarettes did you smoke?	0 1–10 11–20 21–30 31–40	0 1–10 11–20 21–30 31–40	0 1–10 11–20 21–30 31–40	0 1–10 11–20 21–30 31–40	0 1–10 11–20 21–30 31–40	0 1–10 11–20 21–30 31–40	0 1–10 11–20 21–30 31–40	0 1–10 11–20 21–30 31–40	0 1–10 11–20 21–30 31–40	0 1–10 11–20 21–30 31–40	0 1–10 11–20 21–30 31–40	0 1–10 11–20 21–30 31–40	0 1–10 11–20 21–30 31–40	0 1–10 11–20 21–30 31–40
2. How many alcoholic drinks did you have?	0 1–2 3–4 5–6 7–8	0 1–2 3–4 5–6 7–8	0 1–2 3–4 5–6 7–8	0 1–2 3–4 5–6 7–8	0 1–2 3–4 5–6 7–8	0 1–2 3–4 5–6 7–8	0 1–2 3–4 5–6 7–8	0 1–2 3–4 5–6 7–8	0 1–2 3–4 5–6 7–8	0 1–2 3–4 5–6 7–8	0 1–2 3–4 5–6 7–8	0 1–2 3–4 5–6 7–8	0 1–2 3–4 5–6 7–8	0 1–2 3–4 5–6 7–8
3. How many times did you use other drugs?	0 1–2 3–4 5–6 7–8	0 1–2 3–4 5–6 7–8	0 1–2 3–4 5–6 7–8	0 1–2 3–4 5–6 7–8	0 1–2 3–4 5–6 7–8	0 1–2 3–4 5–6 7–8	0 1–2 3–4 5–6 7–8	0 1–2 3–4 5–6 7–8	0 1–2 3–4 5–6 7–8	0 1–2 3–4 5–6 7–8	0 1–2 3–4 5–6 7–8	0 1–2 3–4 5–6 7–8	0 1–2 3–4 5–6 7–8	0 1–2 3–4 5–6 7–8
4. How many times did you use more than you intended?	0 1–2 3–4 5–6 7–8	0 1–2 3–4 5–6 7–8	0 1–2 3–4 5–6 7–8	0 1–2 3–4 5–6 7–8	0 1–2 3–4 5–6 7–8	0 1–2 3–4 5–6 7–8	0 1–2 3–4 5–6 7–8	0 1–2 3–4 5–6 7–8	0 1–2 3–4 5–6 7–8	0 1–2 3–4 5–6 7–8	0 1–2 3–4 5–6 7–8	0 1–2 3–4 5–6 7–8	0 1–2 3–4 5–6 7–8	0 1–2 3–4 5–6 7–8
5. How many times did you feel angry, depressed, or in a bad mood afterwards?	0 1 2 3 4	0 1 2 3 4	0 1 2 3 4	0 1 2 3 4	0 1 2 3 4	0 1 2 3 4	0 1 2 3 4	0 1 2 3 4	0 1 2 3 4	0 1 2 3 4	0 1 2 3 4	0 1 2 3 4	0 1 2 3 4	0 1 2 3 4
6. How many times did your use get you into trouble at school?	0 1 2 3 4	0 1 2 3 4	0 1 2 3 4	0 1 2 3 4	0 1 2 3 4	0 1 2 3 4	0 1 2 3 4	0 1 2 3 4	0 1 2 3 4	0 1 2 3 4	0 1 2 3 4	0 1 2 3 4	0 1 2 3 4	0 1 2 3 4
7. How many times did your use cause problems with family or friends?	0 1 2 3 4	0 1 2 3 4	0 1 2 3 4	0 1 2 3 4	0 1 2 3 4	0 1 2 3 4	0 1 2 3 4	0 1 2 3 4	0 1 2 3 4	0 1 2 3 4	0 1 2 3 4	0 1 2 3 4	0 1 2 3 4	0 1 2 3 4
MY DRUG-USE CONTROL GOAL FOR THE WEEK														
DID I ACHIEVE MY GOAL FOR THE WEEK?	☐ Yes ☐ Almost ☐ About Half ☐ Missed It							☐ Yes ☐ Almost ☐ About Half ☐ Missed It						

Reconnecting Youth © 2004 Solution Tree

Drug-Use Control Diary
(WEEKS 11–12)

DRUG USE AND CONSEQUENCES	WEEK OF _____							WEEK OF _____						
ON THIS DAY ▶	Sat	Sun	Mon	Tue	Wed	Thu	Fri	Sat	Sun	Mon	Tue	Wed	Thu	Fri
	(Circle the appropriate number or range of numbers.)							*(Circle the appropriate number or range of numbers.)*						
1. How many cigarettes did you smoke?	0 1–10 11–20 21–30 31–40	0 1–10 11–20 21–30 31–40	0 1–10 11–20 21–30 31–40	0 1–10 11–20 21–30 31–40	0 1–10 11–20 21–30 31–40	0 1–10 11–20 21–30 31–40	0 1–10 11–20 21–30 31–40	0 1–10 11–20 21–30 31–40	0 1–10 11–20 21–30 31–40	0 1–10 11–20 21–30 31–40	0 1–10 11–20 21–30 31–40	0 1–10 11–20 21–30 31–40	0 1–10 11–20 21–30 31–40	0 1–10 11–20 21–30 31–40
2. How many alcoholic drinks did you have?	0 1–2 3–4 5–6 7–8	0 1–2 3–4 5–6 7–8	0 1–2 3–4 5–6 7–8	0 1–2 3–4 5–6 7–8	0 1–2 3–4 5–6 7–8	0 1–2 3–4 5–6 7–8	0 1–2 3–4 5–6 7–8	0 1–2 3–4 5–6 7–8	0 1–2 3–4 5–6 7–8	0 1–2 3–4 5–6 7–8	0 1–2 3–4 5–6 7–8	0 1–2 3–4 5–6 7–8	0 1–2 3–4 5–6 7–8	0 1–2 3–4 5–6 7–8
3. How many times did you use other drugs?	0 1–2 3–4 5–6 7–8	0 1–2 3–4 5–6 7–8	0 1–2 3–4 5–6 7–8	0 1–2 3–4 5–6 7–8	0 1–2 3–4 5–6 7–8	0 1–2 3–4 5–6 7–8	0 1–2 3–4 5–6 7–8	0 1–2 3–4 5–6 7–8	0 1–2 3–4 5–6 7–8	0 1–2 3–4 5–6 7–8	0 1–2 3–4 5–6 7–8	0 1–2 3–4 5–6 7–8	0 1–2 3–4 5–6 7–8	0 1–2 3–4 5–6 7–8
4. How many times did you use more than you intended?	0 1–2 3–4 5–6 7–8	0 1–2 3–4 5–6 7–8	0 1–2 3–4 5–6 7–8	0 1–2 3–4 5–6 7–8	0 1–2 3–4 5–6 7–8	0 1–2 3–4 5–6 7–8	0 1–2 3–4 5–6 7–8	0 1–2 3–4 5–6 7–8	0 1–2 3–4 5–6 7–8	0 1–2 3–4 5–6 7–8	0 1–2 3–4 5–6 7–8	0 1–2 3–4 5–6 7–8	0 1–2 3–4 5–6 7–8	0 1–2 3–4 5–6 7–8
5. How many times did you feel angry, depressed, or in a bad mood afterwards?	0 1 2 3 4	0 1 2 3 4	0 1 2 3 4	0 1 2 3 4	0 1 2 3 4	0 1 2 3 4	0 1 2 3 4	0 1 2 3 4	0 1 2 3 4	0 1 2 3 4	0 1 2 3 4	0 1 2 3 4	0 1 2 3 4	0 1 2 3 4
6. How many times did your use get you into trouble at school?	0 1 2 3 4	0 1 2 3 4	0 1 2 3 4	0 1 2 3 4	0 1 2 3 4	0 1 2 3 4	0 1 2 3 4	0 1 2 3 4	0 1 2 3 4	0 1 2 3 4	0 1 2 3 4	0 1 2 3 4	0 1 2 3 4	0 1 2 3 4
7. How many times did your use cause problems with family or friends?	0 1 2 3 4	0 1 2 3 4	0 1 2 3 4	0 1 2 3 4	0 1 2 3 4	0 1 2 3 4	0 1 2 3 4	0 1 2 3 4	0 1 2 3 4	0 1 2 3 4	0 1 2 3 4	0 1 2 3 4	0 1 2 3 4	0 1 2 3 4
MY DRUG-USE CONTROL GOAL FOR THE WEEK														
DID I ACHIEVE MY GOAL FOR THE WEEK?	☐ Yes ☐ About Half			☐ Almost ☐ Missed It				☐ Yes ☐ About Half			☐ Almost ☐ Missed It			

Drug-Use Control Diary

(WEEKS 13–14)

DRUG USE AND CONSEQUENCES	WEEK OF _____							WEEK OF _____						
ON THIS DAY ▶	**Sat**	**Sun**	**Mon**	**Tue**	**Wed**	**Thu**	**Fri**	**Sat**	**Sun**	**Mon**	**Tue**	**Wed**	**Thu**	**Fri**
	(Circle the appropriate number or range of numbers.)							*(Circle the appropriate number or range of numbers.)*						
1. How many cigarettes did you smoke?	0 1–10 11–20 21–30 31–40	0 1–10 11–20 21–30 31–40	0 1–10 11–20 21–30 31–40	0 1–10 11–20 21–30 31–40	0 1–10 11–20 21–30 31–40	0 1–10 11–20 21–30 31–40	0 1–10 11–20 21–30 31–40	0 1–10 11–20 21–30 31–40	0 1–10 11–20 21–30 31–40	0 1–10 11–20 21–30 31–40	0 1–10 11–20 21–30 31–40	0 1–10 11–20 21–30 31–40	0 1–10 11–20 21–30 31–40	0 1–10 11–20 21–30 31–40
2. How many alcoholic drinks did you have?	0 1–2 3–4 5–6 7–8	0 1–2 3–4 5–6 7–8	0 1–2 3–4 5–6 7–8	0 1–2 3–4 5–6 7–8	0 1–2 3–4 5–6 7–8	0 1–2 3–4 5–6 7–8	0 1–2 3–4 5–6 7–8	0 1–2 3–4 5–6 7–8	0 1–2 3–4 5–6 7–8	0 1–2 3–4 5–6 7–8	0 1–2 3–4 5–6 7–8	0 1–2 3–4 5–6 7–8	0 1–2 3–4 5–6 7–8	0 1–2 3–4 5–6 7–8
3. How many times did you use other drugs?	0 1–2 3–4 5–6 7–8	0 1–2 3–4 5–6 7–8	0 1–2 3–4 5–6 7–8	0 1–2 3–4 5–6 7–8	0 1–2 3–4 5–6 7–8	0 1–2 3–4 5–6 7–8	0 1–2 3–4 5–6 7–8	0 1–2 3–4 5–6 7–8	0 1–2 3–4 5–6 7–8	0 1–2 3–4 5–6 7–8	0 1–2 3–4 5–6 7–8	0 1–2 3–4 5–6 7–8	0 1–2 3–4 5–6 7–8	0 1–2 3–4 5–6 7–8
4. How many times did you use more than you intended?	0 1–2 3–4 5–6 7–8	0 1–2 3–4 5–6 7–8	0 1–2 3–4 5–6 7–8	0 1–2 3–4 5–6 7–8	0 1–2 3–4 5–6 7–8	0 1–2 3–4 5–6 7–8	0 1–2 3–4 5–6 7–8	0 1–2 3–4 5–6 7–8	0 1–2 3–4 5–6 7–8	0 1–2 3–4 5–6 7–8	0 1–2 3–4 5–6 7–8	0 1–2 3–4 5–6 7–8	0 1–2 3–4 5–6 7–8	0 1–2 3–4 5–6 7–8
5. How many times did you feel angry, depressed, or in a bad mood afterwards?	0 1 2 3 4	0 1 2 3 4	0 1 2 3 4	0 1 2 3 4	0 1 2 3 4	0 1 2 3 4	0 1 2 3 4	0 1 2 3 4	0 1 2 3 4	0 1 2 3 4	0 1 2 3 4	0 1 2 3 4	0 1 2 3 4	0 1 2 3 4
6. How many times did your use get you into trouble at school?	0 1 2 3 4	0 1 2 3 4	0 1 2 3 4	0 1 2 3 4	0 1 2 3 4	0 1 2 3 4	0 1 2 3 4	0 1 2 3 4	0 1 2 3 4	0 1 2 3 4	0 1 2 3 4	0 1 2 3 4	0 1 2 3 4	0 1 2 3 4
7. How many times did your use cause problems with family or friends?	0 1 2 3 4	0 1 2 3 4	0 1 2 3 4	0 1 2 3 4	0 1 2 3 4	0 1 2 3 4	0 1 2 3 4	0 1 2 3 4	0 1 2 3 4	0 1 2 3 4	0 1 2 3 4	0 1 2 3 4	0 1 2 3 4	0 1 2 3 4
MY DRUG-USE CONTROL GOAL FOR THE WEEK														
DID I ACHIEVE MY GOAL FOR THE WEEK?	❏ Yes ❏ About Half		❏ Almost ❏ Missed It					❏ Yes ❏ About Half		❏ Almost ❏ Missed It				

MONITORING TOOLS

Drug-Use Control Diary
(WEEKS 15–16)

DRUG USE AND CONSEQUENCES	WEEK OF _____							WEEK OF _____						
ON THIS DAY ▶	Sat	Sun	Mon	Tue	Wed	Thu	Fri	Sat	Sun	Mon	Tue	Wed	Thu	Fri
	(Circle the appropriate number or range of numbers.)							*(Circle the appropriate number or range of numbers.)*						
1. How many cigarettes did you smoke?	0 1–10 11–20 21–30 31–40	0 1–10 11–20 21–30 31–40	0 1–10 11–20 21–30 31–40	0 1–10 11–20 21–30 31–40	0 1–10 11–20 21–30 31–40	0 1–10 11–20 21–30 31–40	0 1–10 11–20 21–30 31–40	0 1–10 11–20 21–30 31–40	0 1–10 11–20 21–30 31–40	0 1–10 11–20 21–30 31–40	0 1–10 11–20 21–30 31–40	0 1–10 11–20 21–30 31–40	0 1–10 11–20 21–30 31–40	0 1–10 11–20 21–30 31–40
2. How many alcoholic drinks did you have?	0 1–2 3–4 5–6 7–8	0 1–2 3–4 5–6 7–8	0 1–2 3–4 5–6 7–8	0 1–2 3–4 5–6 7–8	0 1–2 3–4 5–6 7–8	0 1–2 3–4 5–6 7–8	0 1–2 3–4 5–6 7–8	0 1–2 3–4 5–6 7–8	0 1–2 3–4 5–6 7–8	0 1–2 3–4 5–6 7–8	0 1–2 3–4 5–6 7–8	0 1–2 3–4 5–6 7–8	0 1–2 3–4 5–6 7–8	0 1–2 3–4 5–6 7–8
3. How many times did you use other drugs?	0 1–2 3–4 5–6 7–8	0 1–2 3–4 5–6 7–8	0 1–2 3–4 5–6 7–8	0 1–2 3–4 5–6 7–8	0 1–2 3–4 5–6 7–8	0 1–2 3–4 5–6 7–8	0 1–2 3–4 5–6 7–8	0 1–2 3–4 5–6 7–8	0 1–2 3–4 5–6 7–8	0 1–2 3–4 5–6 7–8	0 1–2 3–4 5–6 7–8	0 1–2 3–4 5–6 7–8	0 1–2 3–4 5–6 7–8	0 1–2 3–4 5–6 7–8
4. How many times did you use more than you intended?	0 1–2 3–4 5–6 7–8	0 1–2 3–4 5–6 7–8	0 1–2 3–4 5–6 7–8	0 1–2 3–4 5–6 7–8	0 1–2 3–4 5–6 7–8	0 1–2 3–4 5–6 7–8	0 1–2 3–4 5–6 7–8	0 1–2 3–4 5–6 7–8	0 1–2 3–4 5–6 7–8	0 1–2 3–4 5–6 7–8	0 1–2 3–4 5–6 7–8	0 1–2 3–4 5–6 7–8	0 1–2 3–4 5–6 7–8	0 1–2 3–4 5–6 7–8
5. How many times did you feel angry, depressed, or in a bad mood afterwards?	0 1 2 3 4	0 1 2 3 4	0 1 2 3 4	0 1 2 3 4	0 1 2 3 4	0 1 2 3 4	0 1 2 3 4	0 1 2 3 4	0 1 2 3 4	0 1 2 3 4	0 1 2 3 4	0 1 2 3 4	0 1 2 3 4	0 1 2 3 4
6. How many times did your use get you into trouble at school?	0 1 2 3 4	0 1 2 3 4	0 1 2 3 4	0 1 2 3 4	0 1 2 3 4	0 1 2 3 4	0 1 2 3 4	0 1 2 3 4	0 1 2 3 4	0 1 2 3 4	0 1 2 3 4	0 1 2 3 4	0 1 2 3 4	0 1 2 3 4
7. How many times did your use cause problems with family or friends?	0 1 2 3 4	0 1 2 3 4	0 1 2 3 4	0 1 2 3 4	0 1 2 3 4	0 1 2 3 4	0 1 2 3 4	0 1 2 3 4	0 1 2 3 4	0 1 2 3 4	0 1 2 3 4	0 1 2 3 4	0 1 2 3 4	0 1 2 3 4
MY DRUG-USE CONTROL GOAL FOR THE WEEK														
DID I ACHIEVE MY GOAL FOR THE WEEK?	❑ Yes ❑ About Half			❑ Almost ❑ Missed It				❑ Yes ❑ About Half			❑ Almost ❑ Missed It			

Drug-Use Control Diary

(WEEKS 17–18)

DRUG USE AND CONSEQUENCES	WEEK OF _____							WEEK OF _____						
ON THIS DAY ▶	Sat	Sun	Mon	Tue	Wed	Thu	Fri	Sat	Sun	Mon	Tue	Wed	Thu	Fri
	(Circle the appropriate number or range of numbers.)							*(Circle the appropriate number or range of numbers.)*						
1. How many cigarettes did you smoke?	0 1–10 11–20 21–30 31–40	0 1–10 11–20 21–30 31–40	0 1–10 11–20 21–30 31–40	0 1–10 11–20 21–30 31–40	0 1–10 11–20 21–30 31–40	0 1–10 11–20 21–30 31–40	0 1–10 11–20 21–30 31–40	0 1–10 11–20 21–30 31–40	0 1–10 11–20 21–30 31–40	0 1–10 11–20 21–30 31–40	0 1–10 11–20 21–30 31–40	0 1–10 11–20 21–30 31–40	0 1–10 11–20 21–30 31–40	0 1–10 11–20 21–30 31–40
2. How many alcoholic drinks did you have?	0 1–2 3–4 5–6 7–8	0 1–2 3–4 5–6 7–8	0 1–2 3–4 5–6 7–8	0 1–2 3–4 5–6 7–8	0 1–2 3–4 5–6 7–8	0 1–2 3–4 5–6 7–8	0 1–2 3–4 5–6 7–8	0 1–2 3–4 5–6 7–8	0 1–2 3–4 5–6 7–8	0 1–2 3–4 5–6 7–8	0 1–2 3–4 5–6 7–8	0 1–2 3–4 5–6 7–8	0 1–2 3–4 5–6 7–8	0 1–2 3–4 5–6 7–8
3. How many times did you use other drugs?	0 1–2 3–4 5–6 7–8	0 1–2 3–4 5–6 7–8	0 1–2 3–4 5–6 7–8	0 1–2 3–4 5–6 7–8	0 1–2 3–4 5–6 7–8	0 1–2 3–4 5–6 7–8	0 1–2 3–4 5–6 7–8	0 1–2 3–4 5–6 7–8	0 1–2 3–4 5–6 7–8	0 1–2 3–4 5–6 7–8	0 1–2 3–4 5–6 7–8	0 1–2 3–4 5–6 7–8	0 1–2 3–4 5–6 7–8	0 1–2 3–4 5–6 7–8
4. How many times did you use more than you intended?	0 1–2 3–4 5–6 7–8	0 1–2 3–4 5–6 7–8	0 1–2 3–4 5–6 7–8	0 1–2 3–4 5–6 7–8	0 1–2 3–4 5–6 7–8	0 1–2 3–4 5–6 7–8	0 1–2 3–4 5–6 7–8	0 1–2 3–4 5–6 7–8	0 1–2 3–4 5–6 7–8	0 1–2 3–4 5–6 7–8	0 1–2 3–4 5–6 7–8	0 1–2 3–4 5–6 7–8	0 1–2 3–4 5–6 7–8	0 1–2 3–4 5–6 7–8
5. How many times did you feel angry, depressed, or in a bad mood afterwards?	0 1 2 3 4	0 1 2 3 4	0 1 2 3 4	0 1 2 3 4	0 1 2 3 4	0 1 2 3 4	0 1 2 3 4	0 1 2 3 4	0 1 2 3 4	0 1 2 3 4	0 1 2 3 4	0 1 2 3 4	0 1 2 3 4	0 1 2 3 4
6. How many times did your use get you into trouble at school?	0 1 2 3 4	0 1 2 3 4	0 1 2 3 4	0 1 2 3 4	0 1 2 3 4	0 1 2 3 4	0 1 2 3 4	0 1 2 3 4	0 1 2 3 4	0 1 2 3 4	0 1 2 3 4	0 1 2 3 4	0 1 2 3 4	0 1 2 3 4
7. How many times did your use cause problems with family or friends?	0 1 2 3 4	0 1 2 3 4	0 1 2 3 4	0 1 2 3 4	0 1 2 3 4	0 1 2 3 4	0 1 2 3 4	0 1 2 3 4	0 1 2 3 4	0 1 2 3 4	0 1 2 3 4	0 1 2 3 4	0 1 2 3 4	0 1 2 3 4
MY DRUG-USE CONTROL GOAL FOR THE WEEK														
DID I ACHIEVE MY GOAL FOR THE WEEK?	❏ Yes ❏ About Half			❏ Almost ❏ Missed It				❏ Yes ❏ About Half			❏ Almost ❏ Missed It			

Self-Esteem
Enhancement

What Am I?

Here's a riddle for you. What is invisible but is something you see? What cannot speak but is something you hear? What has no form but is something you feel?

Here are some clues. Only you can see it . . . hear it . . . or feel it.

Another clue: think of a movie screen and put it in your mind. Now think of how you get through the day—you do a lot, don't you? Talk, act, think. Maybe more talking and less acting, or less talking and more thinking. At the end of the day, you can replay what happened on the movie screen in your mind. What do you think about what you see?

Here's a final clue. Only you can change it.

If you're still looking for an answer, ask yourself these questions: How do I see myself? What do I think about myself? How do I feel about myself?

Your answers will help you understand the thing that can't be seen, but is a big part of who you are: your self-esteem.

SELF-ESTEEM

Self-Esteem: An Overview

Definition: Positive self-esteem means knowing and appreciating yourself.

Benefits of Positive Self-Esteem

- Makes you feel better

- Allows you to be yourself

- Helps you stand up for yourself

- Frees up energies to let you do what is important to you

- Helps you accept criticism and turn it into self-improvement

- Allows you to help others

- Allows you to have quality relationships with others

To Improve Your Self-Esteem

- Practice positive self-talk.

- Be accurate in self-appraisal.

- Accept responsibility for your actions.

- Show care and concern for others.

- Accept and handle criticism.

- Set goals for self-improvement.

RY's Best Self

How do we show "care and concern" when we are at our best?

What does our group "look like" at our best?

What does our group "feel like" at our best?

SELF-ESTEEM

What does our group "sound like" when we are at our best?

1. Inside the group hands, write the words that describe us at our best.

2. In the area outside of the hands, write words that describe those things we do that distract us from being "Our Best Self."

Self-Esteem Checklist

❏ I am practicing positive self-talk.

❏ I am being accurate in my self-appraisal.

❏ I am accepting responsibility for my actions.

❏ I am showing care and concern for others.

❏ I am accepting and handling criticism.

❏ I am setting goals for self-improvement.

"Hugs," Not "Slugs"

Helping Yourself With Self-Esteem

SELF-ESTEEM

 Hugs

 Slugs

Hugs	Slugs
♡ Positive Self-Talk	⚡ Making Excuses
♡ Liking Yourself	⚡ Disliking Yourself
♡ Making an Effort	⚡ Giving Up
♡ Good Self-Care	⚡ Poor Self-Care
♡ Accepting Personal Responsibility	⚡ Put-downs! Negative Self-Talk!

Adapted from *Defending Yourself Against Criticism: The Slug Manual* by Jennifer James. Copyright © 1984, 1990, 1993 by Jennifer James, ISBN: 1-55704-179-2. Reprinted by permission of Newmarket Press, 18 East 48th Street, New York, NY 10017. www.newmarketpress.com

"Hugs," Not "Slugs"

Helping Others With Self-Esteem

 Hugs

 Slugs

♡ Showing Care and Concern

⚡ Put-downs

♡ Praise— "Awesome, Dude!"

⚡ Rejecting Differences

♡ Encouragement

⚡ Not Caring

♡ Respecting Differences Forgiving

⚡ Blaming

♡ I like to hear your opinion! You're really smart and have guts!

⚡ It's all your fault! What a loser!

Adapted from *Defending Yourself Against Criticism: The Slug Manual* by Jennifer James. Copyright © 1984, 1990, 1993 by Jennifer James, ISBN: 1-55704-179-2. Reprinted by permission of Newmarket Press, 18 East 48th Street, New York, NY 10017. www.newmarketpress.com

Giving and Receiving Positive Feedback (Verbal Hugs)

Person 1: Choose a situation where you could use some positive support (a verbal hug). Briefly share the situation.

Person 2: Respond with a verbal hug—a statement that shows "care and concern" for your partner.

Person 1: Share how you would feel if you were given this kind of verbal hug from another group member.

Partners: Discuss what this same situation would be like if a slug had been given rather than a hug.

Reverse roles, and repeat the practice.

SELF-ESTEEM

Giving and Receiving
Helpful Criticism in a Group

Work in groups of three to complete this activity.

Person 1: **Choose a situation where you might need some helpful criticism.** Briefly describe the situation in one or two sentences.

Person 2: **Briefly give Person 1 some helpful criticism.** (Be helpful—show care and concern. Talk about the specific behavior or problem. Do not put down the person.)

Person 1: **Briefly respond to the criticism.** If appropriate, accept responsibility for your actions. Express appreciation for the care and concern.

Person 3: **Give feedback to Person 2 about his or her helpful criticism.** What did you like about what was said? **Then give feedback to Person 1 about how he or she handled the helpful criticism.** What did you like about how it was handled?

Repeat the process. Each person takes a turn being Person 1, Person 2, and Person 3.

Report back to the large group.

◎ What are good ways to give helpful criticism?

◎ What are good ways to receive helpful criticism?

Booster: Brown Bragging It!

Write positive statements about your recent achievements using the file cards and stickers that have been provided. Put one statement on each file card, decorate the file card with stickers, and place it in your "brown bag."

Examples of Positive Statements of Achievement

- I have excellent attendance in RY.

- I am a good group member who shows care and concern for others.

- My attitude toward school is really improving.

- I received a B+ on my English paper.

- I am now doing homework almost every day.

- I am working hard at managing my mood.

- I am getting along better with my parents.

- I am setting goals and achieving them here at school.

- I continue to be drug free.

- I am thinking carefully about the decisions I make regarding drug use.

Place in your brown bag any other objects you brought to class that represent recent achievements.

Be prepared to share the contents of your brown bag with the group. As you share, talk about the effects your achievements have had on your self-esteem.

SELF-ESTEEM

Booster: Praise Waves

1. Write a **NOTE** to the person on your left. Tell this person something you really like or respect about him or her. When everyone is done, deliver your note.

2. Make a positive **BOOKMARK** for the person two seats down from you on your left. Say something nice about the recipient on the bookmark. (For example, "Your laugh is wonderful" or "You really share good ideas in the group.") Color and decorate your bookmark. When everyone is done, deliver your bookmark.

3. Write a **NOTE OF PRAISE** to the person three seats down from you on your left. Give this person praise for improvement on a program goal he or she has made so far during group (for example, improved attendance, better attitude, more participation during group). Add a sticker or drawing to the note. When everyone is done, deliver your note.

4. Make a **DRAWING** for the person four seats down from you on your left. Include verbal hugs for the recipient—compliments on things the person has said or done during group. (For example, "I really appreciate the advice you gave me yesterday" or "Your support during group earlier this week was great.") Color or add stickers to your drawing. When everyone is done, deliver your drawing.

About Affirmations

"Affirm" means TO MAKE FIRM.

An affirmation MAKES FIRM something positive about yourself.

When you write affirmations . . .

 Stay in the present, **not** the future. Example: "I *am* a capable person," (**not** "I *will* be a capable person.")

 Affirm what you are, **not** what you *are not*. Example: "I *am* drug free," (**not** "I *am not* on drugs.")

 Believe your affirmation!

Be sure to . . .

✎ Keep the statement short and simple.

✎ Choose an affirmation that feels right for you. Ask yourself, "Does this affirmation make me feel positive and supported?" "Does this affirmation make me feel free?" If not, change the words or find another affirmation until it feels right.

Excerpted from *Creative Visualization* by Shakti Gawain © 2002. Used with permission from New World Library, Novato, CA 94949. www.newworldlibrary.com

SELF-ESTEEM

Affirmations About Our Group

(For example: "We care about each other.")

1 _____

2 _____

3 _____

4 _____

5 _____

Affirmations About Me

(For example: "I am a capable person.")

1 _____

2 _____

3 _____

4 _____

5 _____

An Affirmation for

SELF-ESTEEM

- Write an affirmation that fits the person sitting next to you on your left.

- Make it positive! Make it supportive!

- Now exchange affirmations, and place the affirmation you received here in your book.

Booster: Sample Self-Esteem Tree

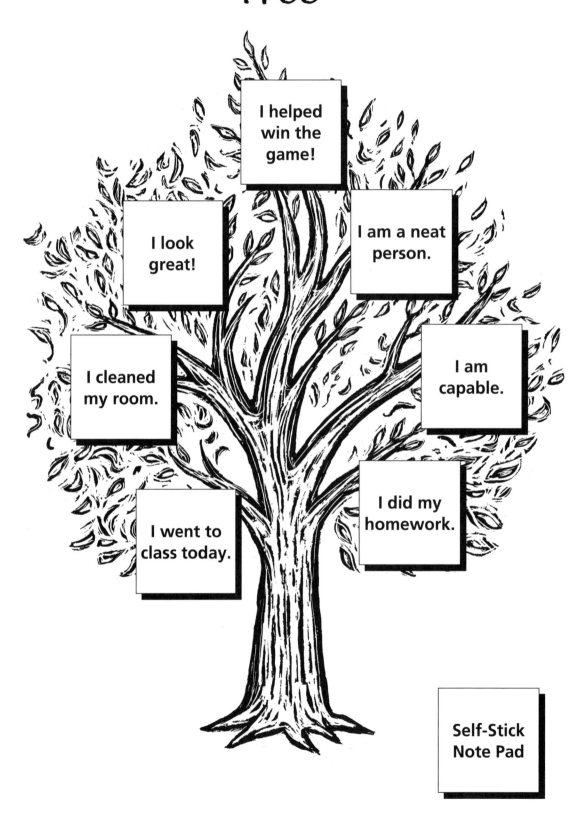

CONTRACT TO PRACTICE

Using Visualization to Relieve Stress and Enhance Self-Esteem

1 Identify a recent situation where you could have used visualization to relax or make you feel good about yourself.

_____

_____

_____

2 Identify a situation that will probably occur in the next 24 hours that will be stressful for you. Briefly describe the situation.

_____

_____

_____

3 Identify and briefly describe a relaxing, positive image you are willing to visualize to help you handle the situation described in item 2 above.

_____

_____

_____

Be prepared to share this information with the group. You will have an opportunity at our next group meeting to discuss how visualization worked for you.

Critical Features of Survivors!

Survivors are people who . . .

🌴 have a lot of determination

🌴 _____

🌴 _____

🌴 _____

🌴 _____

🌴 _____

🌴 _____

🌴 _____

🌴 _____

CONTRACT TO PRACTICE

Using a Personal Strength

Write down a stressful situation that is likely to occur for you in the next 24 hours.

_____

_____

_____

What personal strength will you use to help you cope with this situation?

_____

_____

_____

How could this strength of yours benefit the group?

_____

_____

_____

How might you benefit from your partner's strength in our group?

_____

_____

_____

My Best Self

After listening to the group visualization exercise, write below the specific images or feelings you experienced.

◎ _____

◎ _____

◎ _____

◎ _____

◎ _____

Write below one or two specific images or feelings from your list above that you would like to see come true in your life.

◎ _____

◎ _____

What are the first steps you will take toward having one of these goals come true in your life?

◎ _____

◎ _____

◎ _____

Share with the group your goal and your plan for starting to achieve it.

Booster: Sample Coat of Arms

On the next page, create your own personal coat of arms that honors who you are and what you value. Use pictures, words, or both to fill in each of the six areas on your shield.

1. What is something you do very well?

2. What is something you're trying to do better?

3. What is one value—a deep commitment—that you believe in strongly?

4. What material possession means a lot to you?

5. What one thing can other people do to make you happy?

6. What three words could become your personal motto or words to live by?

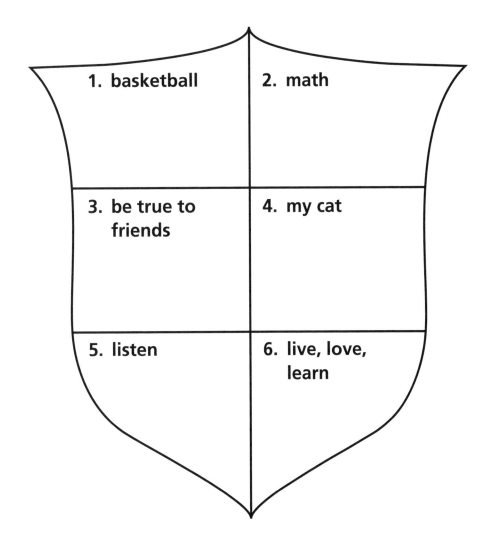

SELF-ESTEEM

Adapted from *In Search of Values: Thirty-one Strategies for Finding Out What Really Matters to You* by Dr. Sidney B. Simon. Copyright © 1993 by Sidney B. Simon. By permission of Warner Books, Inc.

(continued)

Booster: Coat of Arms

Create your own personal coat of arms that honors who you are and what you value. Use pictures, words, or both to fill in each of the six areas on your shield.

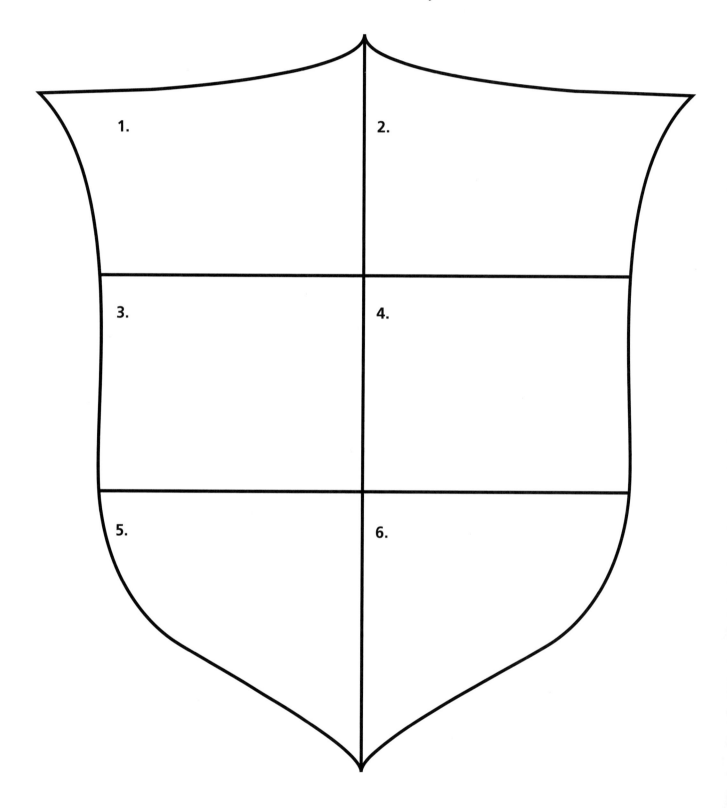

Snap! Zap!

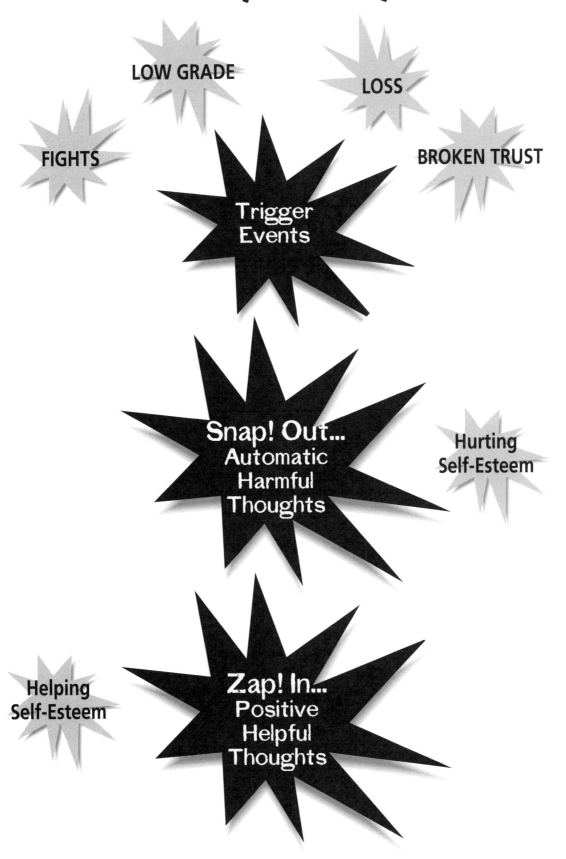

SELF-ESTEEM

My Typical Trigger Events

Write below examples of typical "trigger events" that occur in your life (at school, at home, with friends) that cause harmful thoughts to automatically "flash" through your head.

🔥 _____

🔥 _____

🔥 _____

🔥 _____

SNAP! These Out!

My Automatic Harmful Thoughts

Write below examples of automatic harmful thoughts that flash through your head when a "trigger event" occurs in your life.

✸ _____

✸ _____

✸ _____

ZAP! These In!

My Helpful Replacement Thoughts

Write below examples of helpful replacement thoughts that will help you handle the trigger event in a positive way.

✸ _____

✸ _____

✸ _____

CONTRACT TO PRACTICE

Interrupting Automatic Thoughts

In the next 24 hours, I will practice the Snap! Zap! strategy.

1. Identify a "trigger event" that is likely to occur in the next 24 hours. Briefly describe this event.

   _____

   _____

   _____

2. Identify harmful thoughts that tend to occur automatically when this "trigger event" occurs. Write these harmful thoughts below.

   _____

   _____

   _____

3. **Snap!** out or interrupt these harmful thoughts!

4. **Zap!** in or replace the harmful thoughts with helpful thoughts. Write your helpful thoughts below.

   _____

   _____

   _____

We may not be able to control when a trigger event occurs, but we *can* control our thoughts and our reactions.

Booster:
Pessimist Versus Optimist

Directions

1. Work in pairs to develop a role play that can be shared with the group.

2. Choose one of the role plays written below or develop your own role play.

3. One person is the **pessimist,** and the second person is the **optimist**.

4. The optimist shares the situation with the group, and then the role play begins.

5. The pessimist reacts to the situation by saying aloud the thoughts that will likely hurt his or her self-esteem.

6. The optimist immediately counters by saying aloud the positive thoughts that help the pessimist's self-esteem.

7. Change roles, and repeat the process with a different role play.

Role-Play Situations

◎ You made plans to go to a concert with a friend. At the last minute, your friend tells you he or she also invited someone who you really don't like, even though your friend knows you don't like this person.

◎ Your parents have made vacation plans without discussing them with you. You've been told that you have to go even though you already made plans of your own.

◎ A friend let you borrow a piece of valuable stereo equipment, which you accidentally broke. Though you've agreed to pay for the equipment over time, the friend has stopped talking to you.

◎ For the first time in a long time, you put effort into a paper for English class. You're anticipating a high grade. When you get your paper back, it's covered with red ink, and your grade is a C.

◎ After a long, boring weekend, you return to school Monday morning and learn that a group of friends had a fantastic party over the weekend that no one told you about.

Evaluating Last Semester's Grades and Attendance

In the space below, write areas where you had your best success last semester (for example, attitude, grades, attendance, specific subjects).

◎ _____

◎ _____

◎ _____

◎ _____

◎ _____

Now identify areas where you were less successful last semester (for example, attitude, grades, attendance, specific subjects).

◎ _____

◎ _____

◎ _____

◎ _____

◎ _____

Be prepared to share with the group the areas where you succeeded, the areas where you were less successful, and the effects these had on your self-esteem.

SELF-ESTEEM

Removing Barriers to Success

Directions

List barriers to your success in a specific subject. Ask yourself if the barrier is an **attitude** problem ("I can't stand the teacher!"), a **skill** problem ("I'm terrible at word problems in math."), or an **outside stressor** ("I can't concentrate on homework when everyone at home is fighting."). Work with a partner to find a strategy to "remove the barrier." You can use another piece of paper to analyze other subjects.

Subject: _____

Barriers

Attitude Problems

_____

_____

_____

_____

Skill Problems

_____

_____

_____

_____

Stressor Problems

_____

_____

_____

_____

Strategies

My New Attitudes

_____

_____

_____

_____

Skills I'll Improve

_____

_____

_____

_____

Solutions to Stressors

_____

_____

_____

_____

CONTRACT TO PRACTICE

Removing a Barrier to My Success

In the next 24 hours, I will focus on the following strategy to remove or decrease at least one barrier to my success:

Specific thoughts I will work on:

SNAP! OUT _____

_____

ZAP! IN _____

_____

Specific actions I will work on:

AVOID the following: _____

DO the following: _____

Note of support and encouragement from my partner:

Booster: Dip Into Your Wellspring

1. Think about your interests, skills, talents, and hobbies—for example, playing a sport, being good with animals, being able to fix something that is broken, singing, dancing, being a good and loyal friend.

2. Using colored markers, fill your well by writing down your interests and talents on self-stick notes and putting them inside the well.

3. Be prepared to share with the group how you could use these interests and talents to achieve greater success in school. (For example, you could use the same self-discipline you use in sports to finish your homework, or you could take the confidence and patience you have to fix something and apply it to your low grade in math.)

Coping With Stress: Unhealthy and Healthy Strategies

List examples of **Unhealthy Strategies** you have used to cope with stress.

_____

_____

_____

_____

_____

SELF-ESTEEM

List examples of **Healthy Strategies** you have used or could use to cope with stress.

★ _____

★ _____

★ _____

★ _____

CONTRACT TO PRACTICE

Using Healthy Coping Strategies

I commit myself to trying the following healthy coping strategies in the next 2 days:

_____

_____

_____

_____

I will check in with _____
if I need support over the next 2 days.

I will definitely call _____
at _____on _____ to see how he or
she did with his or her contract and to share how I did with
my contract.

I will be prepared to share with the group how this went over
the next 3 days.

What Does Depression Look Like?

Draw a picture or an image of what depression looks like and feels like for you. Use color, shapes, words, or any combination. No artistic talent required!

Understanding Depression

As you look at the picture you drew of depression, think about how the following might be connected for you when you slip and slide down into depression.

What typically triggers depression for you?

_____

_____

_____

What do you usually feel or think when you are depressed?

_____

_____

_____

What do you typically do when you are depressed?

_____

_____

_____

What helps you begin to feel less depressed?

_____

_____

_____

Tracking Emotional Spirals

Feel unhappy	**Feel great**
⬇	⬆
Spend more time alone	Do well in school
⬇	⬆
Feel depressed	Feel even better
⬇	⬆
Become less active	Have fun with friends
⬇	⬆
Do even less	Feel good
⬇	⬆
Feel even more depressed	Do something successfully

SELF-ESTEEM

Strategies to Reverse Downward Spirals

- ◉ Eliminate negative self-talk.
- ◉ Call a friend.
- ◉ Think positively.
- ◉ Look on my list for fun things to do.
- ◉ Keep up the good work!

Reconnecting Youth © 2004 Solution Tree

Reversing Downward Emotional Spirals

Select one or more strategies you will use for a week to reverse downward emotional spirals if and when they occur. Write these below.

🌀 _____

🌀 _____

🌀 _____

🌀 _____

🌀 _____

Exchange workbooks with your partner, and write a note of support and encouragement to use the strategies written above.

Note of support and encouragement from my partner:

Booster: Singing the Blues

1. Take a few minutes to identify and write down every worry and self-doubt that is lurking somewhere inside of you. (For example: "No one likes me," "I'm too heavy," "I'll never have a boyfriend/girlfriend," "I'm dumb"). Write them below.

♫ _____

♫ _____

♫ _____

♫ _____

♫ _____

SELF-ESTEEM

2. Work with a partner to develop a short song, rap, or poem about "The Blues." Be prepared to share your masterpiece with the group.

3. Pairs share their masterpieces!

4. Now work with your partner to rewrite your song, rap, or poem. This time, kick out the blues and sing the new praises of feeling good about yourself! Be prepared to share your new masterpiece with the group.

5. Pairs share their masterpieces!

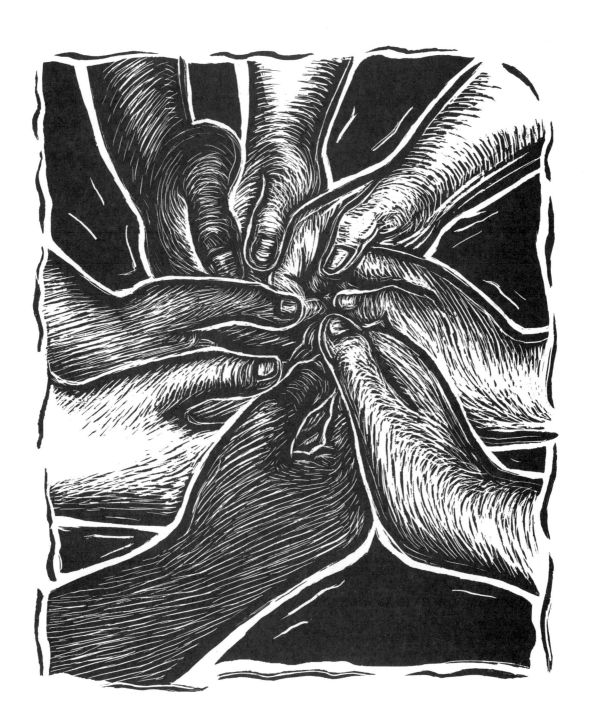

Decision Making

Red Coat, Black Coat? New Coat or No Coat?

You've seen it on TV and heard about it from your friends: the Poly-Pepper red road coat. A sleek red coat with stunning black dots. Kind of like a leopard on ketchup. You need a new coat and have enough money to buy the Poly-Pepper red road coat—or another coat. What do you do next?

- Buy the first road coat you can find?

- Buy a road coat because your friends are wearing Poly-Peppers?

- Look over the road coat and other coats, and choose the best deal?

- Buy a road coat because it matches the shirt you're wearing and the salesperson says you look great?

- Put off buying a coat because you have other things to do and it's not that cold?

- Try on all the coats in the store— twice—but go home without one because it's too hard to choose?

DECISION MAKING

These answers show you different decision-making strategies. What's your strategy? In the next few weeks, you'll take a closer look at how you make decisions. Are your decisions working for you? Or against you?

You'll also learn the STEPS strategy for making better decisions—large or small. Whether you need to buy a new coat or decide what to do next summer, you can take five simple steps to making good decisions.

Decision Making: An Overview

Definition:
A process of selecting from two or more possible options in order to solve a problem or reach a goal.

Planned Decision Making

Group Problems and Goals	Personal Problems and Goals
• Improving School Smarts • Increasing drug-use control • Improving mood management	• Feeling good about myself • Getting something I want • Changing unhealthy habits

DECISION MAKING

Why practice decision making?

- ◎ Gives you **freedom** of choice
- ◎ Gives you **control** over your life
- ◎ Helps you achieve **success** in important things
- ◎ Increases your **self-confidence** and **competence**
- ◎ Gives you **energy** and **reduces stress**

Sample: How Did You Decide?

1. **THINK** about decisions you have made in the last week or month.

2. **WRITE** your decision in the left-hand column below.

3. **RATE** how much thought went into each decision by writing one of the following numbers next to your decision:

    1 = Automatic—did not think about it

    2 = Thought about it a little

    3 = Thought about it a lot

    4 = Thought about it a lot and got information

4. **EVALUATE** each decision as **helpful** or **hurtful** depending on how you think your decision turned out.

My Decisions	How I Decided (1 to 4)	Was It Helpful or Hurtful?
1. _Asked John to go to a party._	2	☑ Helpful ☐ Hurtful
2. _Quit my after-school job._	2	☐ Helpful ☑ Hurtful
3. _Got help for a friend in trouble._	4	☑ Helpful ☐ Hurtful
4. _Skipped school on Tuesday._	1	☐ Helpful ☑ Hurtful

5. Choose one decision from your list above where the result of the decision was **more hurtful** than helpful.

6. Discuss with your partner how you could change the way you made that decision to make it **more helpful.** Be prepared to share your discussion with the group.

How Did You Decide?

1. **THINK** about decisions you have made in the last week or month.

2. **WRITE** your decision in the left-hand column below.

3. **RATE** how much thought went into each decision by writing one of the following numbers next to your decision:

    1 = Automatic—did not think about it

    2 = Thought about it a little

    3 = Thought about it a lot

    4 = Thought about it a lot and got information

4. **EVALUATE** each decision as **helpful** or **hurtful** depending on how you think your decision turned out.

My Decisions	How I Decided (1 to 4)	Was It Helpful or Hurtful?
1._____ _____ _____	_____	❑ Helpful ❑ Hurtful
2._____ _____ _____	_____	❑ Helpful ❑ Hurtful
3._____ _____ _____	_____	❑ Helpful ❑ Hurtful
4._____ _____ _____	_____	❑ Helpful ❑ Hurtful

DECISION MAKING

5. Choose one decision from your list above where the result of the decision was **more hurtful** than helpful.

6. Discuss with your partner how you could change the way you made that decision to make it **more helpful.** Be prepared to share your discussion with the group.

CONTRACT TO PRACTICE

Keeping Track of How You Make Decisions

Keep track of the decisions you make in the next 24 hours that affect your attendance, schoolwork, drug-use control, and mood management.

Rate the amount of thought you gave to each decision, and determine whether the decision was **helpful** or **hurtful**.

1	2	3	4
Automatic, no thought	**A little thought**	**A lot of thought**	**A lot of thought, got information**

My Decision	How I Decided (1 to 4)	Helpful or Hurtful?
Attendance Decision		☐ Helpful ☐ Hurtful
Schoolwork Decision		☐ Helpful ☐ Hurtful
Drug-Use Control Decision		☐ Helpful ☐ Hurtful
Mood Management Decision		☐ Helpful ☐ Hurtful

What insights have you gained about decision making? Be prepared to share your insights with the group.

- _____
- _____

Other Styles of Decision-Making Strategies

A strategy in itself is not good or bad or right or wrong. Different strategies are used at different times for different situations by different people. One study of high school students found the following types of personal decision-making strategies were most commonly used.

Impulsive

Little thought or examination, taking the first alternative: "Leap before you look."

Fatalistic

Letting the environment decide, leaving it up to fate: "It's all in the cards."

Passive

Let someone else decide, following someone else's plans: "Whatever you say."

Delaying

Postponing thought and action: "I'll decide later."

Agonizing

Getting lost in all the information, overwhelmed with analyzing alternatives: "I don't know what to do."

Stuck

The decision-maker accepts responsibility but is unable to act on it: "I can't face it."

Intuitive

A mystical, preconscious choice based on "inner harmony": "It feels right."

Planning

Using a procedure so that the end result is satisfying, a rational approach with a balance between knowledge and emotion: "I'll weigh all the facts."

DECISION MAKING

STEPS to Planned Decision Making

Stop — Take a deep breath. Count to 10. Calm down! Don't act impulsively What will you say to yourself to slow down and think this through?

Think — What are my other options? Brainstorm a list of options: new ones as well as obvious ones.

Evaluate — Which options are helpful? Which options are hurtful? Which options help me achieve my goals? Which one will I try?

Perform — Pick a **helpful** option! What will you do? When? How? Make a to-do list.

Self-Praise — Celebrate your success! You took the STEPS. How will you praise yourself?

Sample Using STEPS

Think of a frequent situation in which you tend to make an impulsive decision that you usually regret later.

Briefly describe the situation:

Join my friends for lunch off campus (and be late for fifth period).

STOP *What will you say to yourself to slow down and think this through?*

Slow down! Don't act impulsively. Think it through. If I go to lunch, I'll be late for fifth period, and the teacher said she'd suspend me from class if I'm tardy again!

THINK *What are your options? (Try to think of new options in addition to the obvious options.)*

1. Go to lunch with my friends.
2. Eat alone in the cafeteria.
3. Ask my friends to bring me back early.
4. Suggest we go someplace closer or quicker.
5. Find out who else needs to be back for fifth period and take two cars.

EVALUATE *Which options are helpful? Which options are hurtful?*

Helpful: 3—Ask my friends to bring me back early.
4—Suggest we go someplace closer or quicker.
5—Find out who else needs to be back for fifth period and take two cars.

Hurtful: 1—Go to lunch and be late for fifth period.
2—Eat alone in the cafeteria.

PERFORM *What will you do? When? How? Make a to-do list if appropriate.*

I will find out who else needs to be back for fifth period and ask if we can take two cars. I'll also suggest that we go someplace closer or quicker. If none of that works, I will eat alone in the cafeteria (or skip lunch), but I'll go to fifth period.

SELF-PRAISE *How will you praise yourself?*

I'm proud that I made a good decision. I won't get kicked out of fifth period!

DECISION MAKING

Using STEPS

Think of a frequent situation in which you tend to make an impulsive decision that you usually regret later.

Briefly describe the situation:

_____

_____

_____

_____

STOP *What will you say to yourself to slow down and think this through?*

_____

_____

_____

_____

THINK *What are your options? (Try to think of new options in addition to the obvious options.)*

1. _____   4. _____

2. _____   5. _____

3. _____   6. _____

(continued)

EVALUATE *Which options are helpful? Which options are hurtful?nn*

	Helpful?	Hurtful?
1. _____	❏	❏
2. _____	❏	❏
3. _____	❏	❏
4. _____	❏	❏
5. _____	❏	❏
6. _____	❏	❏

PERFORM *What will you do? When? How?*

I will . . . _____

When? _____

How? _____

_____

DECISION MAKING

SELF-PRAISE *How will you praise yourself?*

_____

_____

_____

_____

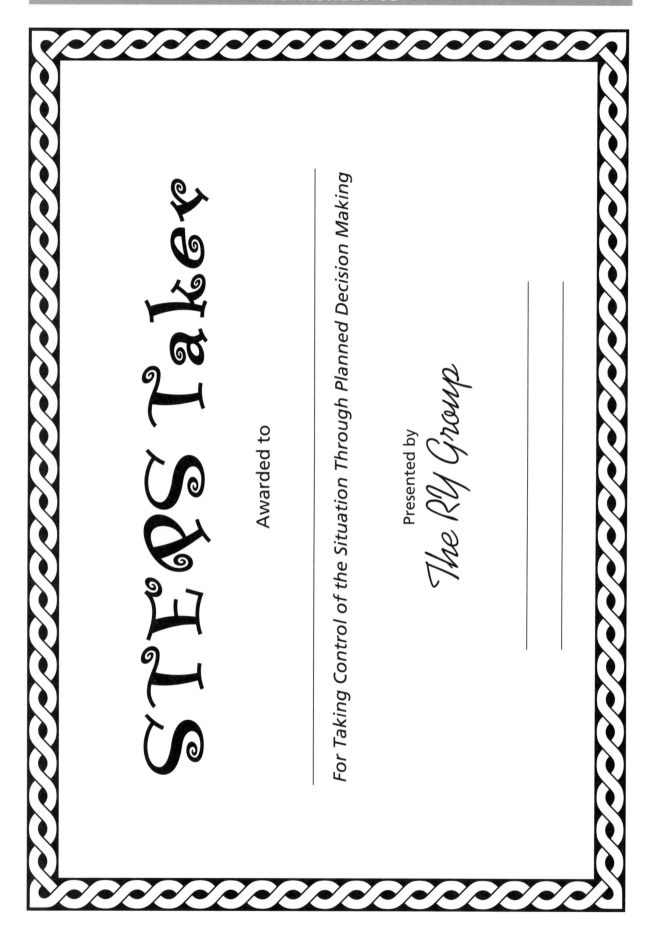

STEPS Taken

Awarded to

_____

For Taking Control of the Situation Through Planned Decision Making

Presented by

The RY Group

_____

CONTRACT TO PRACTICE

Using STEPS

Think of a decision you would like to make in the next 24 hours using the STEPS strategy.

I will use STEPS when I have to decide whether to . . .

_____

_____

_____

_____

STOP. In order to slow down and think this through, I will take a deep breath and then say to myself:

_____

_____

_____

_____

THINK. My options include:

1. _____   4. _____

2. _____   5. _____

3. _____   6. _____

(continued)

CONTRACT TO PRACTICE

EVALUATE *Which options are helpful? Which options are hurtful?*

	Helpful?	Hurtful?
1. _____	❏	❏
2. _____	❏	❏
3. _____	❏	❏
4. _____	❏	❏
5. _____	❏	❏
6. _____	❏	❏

PERFORM *What will I do? When? How?*

I will . . . _____

When? _____

How? _____

_____

SELF-PRAISE *How will I praise myself?*

_____

_____

_____

_____

Be prepared to share with the group how the STEPS process affected the decision you made.

 # RY Goals

Name_____   Date_____

School Attendance ➤ _____
_____

School Achievement ➤ _____
_____

Drug-Use Control ➤ _____
_____

Mood Management ➤ _____
_____

DECISION MAKING

Big RY Goals

The following examples are RY goals that can be achieved within a semester.

Attendance

- I will attend every one of my classes every day (unless I am sick or on a field trip).

- I will not lose credit from any of my classes due to poor attendance.

School Achievement

- I will earn a 2.5 GPA this semester.

- I will improve last semester's GPA of 2.3 to a 3.0 this semester.

Drug-Use Control

- I will remain drug-free this semester.

- I will quit smoking by November 15 and not smoke through the end of the semester.

Mood Management

- I will learn to manage my anger better and decrease the times I hit something or somebody, yell at someone, or lose my temper.

- I will decrease the number of times I feel depressed or discouraged.

Sample RY Goal, Mini-Goals, and To-Do List

Your goal should be

DESIRABLE • SPECIFIC • ACHIEVABLE

RY School Achievement Goal for This Semester

Earn a 2.5 or higher for my semester GPA.

Mini-Goals for RY Goal

- Earn an A in RY and PE.

- Earn a C or better in English and social studies.

- Pass math and science with a D or better.

- Use STEPS to think through my decisions if I am distracted from my goal.

To-Do List

Tasks	Do by	✓ if Done
• Meet with my math teacher and get my assignments.	Today	_____
• Get a math tutor (ask teacher for recommendations).	Today	_____
• Schedule weekly appointments with math tutor.	This week	_____
• Go to math class every day.	Always	_____
• Finish my English book report.	Wednesday	_____
• Study for my social studies test.	Thursday evening	_____

DECISION MAKING

My RY Goal, Mini-Goals, and To-Do List

Your goal should be

DESIRABLE • SPECIFIC • ACHIEVABLE

RY [_____] **Goal for This Semester**

Mini-Goals for RY Goal

- _____
- _____
- _____
- _____

To-Do List

Tasks	**Do by**	**✓ if Done**
• _____	_____	_____
• _____	_____	_____
• _____	_____	_____
• _____	_____	_____
• _____	_____	_____
• _____	_____	_____

CONTRACT TO PRACTICE

Setting Mini-Goals and Accomplishing To-Do Lists

In the next 24 hours, I will work on the following mini-goal:

_____

_____

_____

_____

To achieve my mini-goal, I will take these two steps from my to-do list in the next 24 hours:

1. _____

2. _____

A barrier that might get in my way would be . . .

_____

_____

_____

_____

I will deal with this barrier by . . .

_____

_____

_____

_____

Be prepared to share with the group your progress toward accomplishing your mini-goal.

Reconnecting Youth © 2004 Solution Tree

Sample 24-Hour Time Wheel

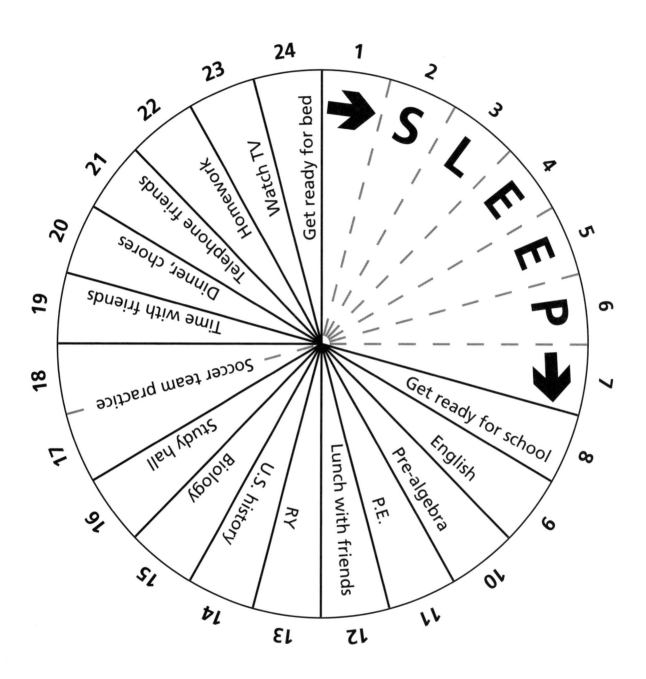

My 24-Hour Time Wheel

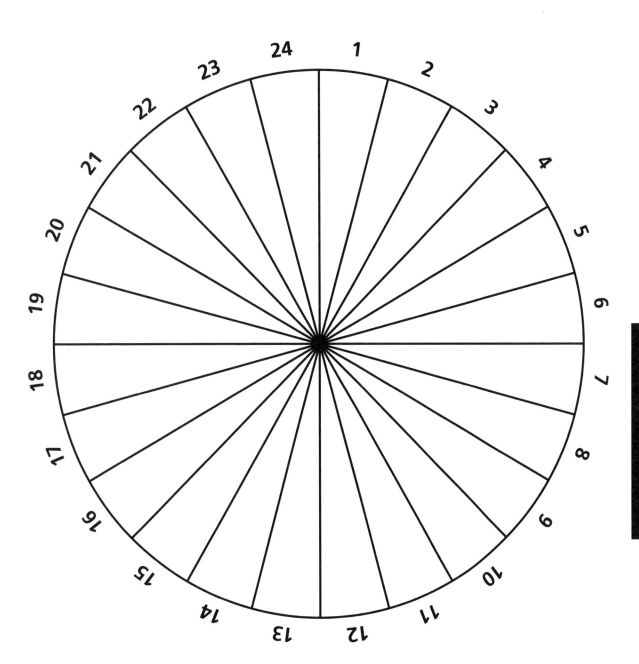

DECISION MAKING

CONTRACT TO PRACTICE

Time Management

1. Exchange **24-Hour Time Wheels** with a partner. Check your partner's wheel to see if it is complete and reasonable. Return the wheel and discuss your observations with your partner.

2. Select one block of time you have scheduled for the next 24 hours to do something that is important to you, but may be difficult to fit in. Write the name of this activity here: _____

3. Discuss with your partner how you will manage your time in order to include your chosen activity. Then complete this sentence:

   I will fit in my activity by managing my time as follows:

   • _____

   • _____

   • _____

   • _____

4. Exchange papers with your partner and write a note of support and encouragement to accomplish the chosen activity.

   Note of support and encouragement from my partner:

Be prepared to follow up with your partner in our next session to see if the important activity was accomplished.

Sample Report Card

Student's Name _____

Date _____ October 10 _____

SUBJECT	TEACHER	NUMBER OF ABSENCES	GRADE	COMMENT CODES
1. English	Adams	7	D	2 All assignments are not turned in. 11 Attendance is affecting the grade.
2. Pre-algebra	Shin	9	D⁻	4 Student is disruptive. 11 Attendance is affecting the grade.
3. P.E.	Day	2	A	3 Student is a pleasure to have in class. 8 Student is doing excellent work.
4. RY	Johnson	0	B	3 Student is a pleasure to have in class. 12 Student is an excellent group member.
5. U.S. history	Jones	5	C	7 Student is progressing satisfactorily. 9 Student's work is improving this quarter.
6. Biology	Alvarez	11	F	4 Student is disruptive. 2 All assignments are not turned in.
7. Study hall	Wilson	11	U	4 Student is disruptive.

DECISION MAKING

Report Card

Your Name _____

Date _____

SUBJECT	TEACHER	NUMBER OF ABSENCES	GRADE	COMMENT CODES
1. _____	_____	_____	◯	_____
2. _____	_____	_____	◯	_____
3. _____	_____	_____	◯	_____
4. _____	_____	_____	◯	_____
5. _____	_____	_____	◯	_____
6. _____	_____	_____	◯	_____
7. _____	_____	_____	◯	_____

Report Card Comment Codes

1. All assignments are turned in.

2. All assignments are not turned in.

3. Student is a pleasure to have in class.

4. Student is disruptive.

5. Subject is hard for student, but he or she makes an effort to learn.

6. Student needs to take initiative and accept responsibility.

7. Student is progressing satisfactorily.

8. Student is doing excellent work.

9. Student's work is improving this quarter.

10. Student's work is declining this quarter.

11. Attendance is affecting the grade.

12. Student is an excellent group member.

13. Test scores need improvement.

14. Other: _____

15. Other: _____

DECISION MAKING

CONTRACT TO PRACTICE

Improving School Achievement

1. A class that I am willing to improve my attitude or behavior in is . . .

   _____

   _____

2. I will work on the following mini-goals to improve in this class:

   • _____

   • _____

   • _____

   • _____

3. A barrier or "trigger" that might get in my way would be . . .

   _____

   _____

24. I will use the following strategy to overcome this barrier:

   _____

   _____

2 Practice using this strategy with your partner.

Be prepared to report on your progress at the next RY session and to grade yourself on your effort to improve this attitude or behavior.

Sample How Can I Improve My Grade?

Name: _____John J. Sample_____

Class: _____Biology_____   Teacher: _____Ms. Alvarez_____

My grade in this class as of _____October 1_____ is __F__.
                                    (Date)   (Grade)

My grade goal for this class by _____November 1_____ is __C__.
                                    (Date)   (Grade)

To Do

Tasks	Do by	✓ if Done
1. Meet with teacher to discuss goal	tomorrow	____
2. Ask teacher to prioritize assignments	tomorrow	____
3. Do first assignment on list	Wednesday	____
4. Ask to change my desk assignment and lab partner	tomorrow	____
5. Spend 30 minutes each day doing biology	begin today	____

John J. Sample 10-03   _Ida Alvarez_ 10-03
(My Signature / Date)   (Teacher's Signature / Date)

Teacher's Comments: _I approve! Good job in taking this initiative. Attached are the priorities for assignments due. I look forward to getting the first assignment tomorrow. We'll change your desk and lab partner. Good luck. I'd like to see you get that C!_

DECISION MAKING

How Can I Improve My Grade?

Name: _____

Class: _____   Teacher: _____

My grade in this class as of _____ is _____.
                                    (Date)   (Grade)

My grade goal for this class by _____ is _____.
                                        (Date)   (Grade)

To Do

Tasks   **Do by**   **✓ if Done**

1. _____   _____   _____

2. _____   _____   _____

3. _____   _____   _____

4. _____   _____   _____

5. _____   _____   _____

_____   _____
(My Signature / Date)   (Teacher's Signature / Date)

Teacher's Comments: _____

_____

_____

_____

_____

CONTRACT TO PRACTICE

Improving My GPA

Think about your GPA goal for the end of this semester. This contract is to accomplish one task in the next 24 hours that moves you toward making that goal.

1. Choose one class for which you developed a to-do list. Choose a class that you are willing to begin working on to reach your goal.

   • Write the name of that class below:

2. In order to meet my GPA goal of _____ for this class, I have selected one item from the to-do list that I will work on during the next 24 hours:

3. One barrier that could keep me from accomplishing this task is . . .

4. I will handle this barrier by . . .

   Work with your partner to practice overcoming this barrier.

5. I will also share my improvement plan with my teacher, _____ _____, today at _____ _____ (time and place) or tomorrow before school starts at _____ (time and place).

Be prepared to report back during our next class on the progress you have made toward accomplishing your task.

Sample Progress Report on Achievement

My GPA first quarter: 1.5

My GPA goal for the end of the semester: 2.0 or higher

Classes	Reporting Times			
1. English	D Estimate Actual	C Goal Actual	Goal Actual	Goal Actual
2. Pre-algebra	F Estimate Actual	D Goal Actual	Goal Actual	Goal Actual
3. P.E.	A Estimate Actual	A Goal Actual	Goal Actual	Goal Actual
4. RY	B Estimate Actual	A Goal Actual	Goal Actual	Goal Actual
5. U.S. history	D Estimate Actual	C Goal Actual	Goal Actual	Goal Actual
6. Biology	F Estimate Actual	D Goal Actual	Goal Actual	Goal Actual
7. Study hall	N Estimate Actual	P Goal Actual	Goal Actual	Goal Actual

Which would give me a GPA of . . .   1.5   _____   _____   _____

4.0	4.0	4.0	4.0
3.8	3.8	3.8	3.8
3.6	3.6	3.6	3.6
3.4	3.4	3.4	3.4
3.2	3.2	3.2	3.2
3.0	3.0	3.0	3.0
2.8	2.8	2.8	2.8
2.6	2.6	2.6	2.6
2.4	2.4	2.4	2.4
2.2	2.2	2.2	2.2
2.0	2.0	2.0	2.0
1.8	1.8	1.8	1.8
(1.6)	1.6	1.6	1.6
1.4	1.4	1.4	1.4
1.2	1.2	1.2	1.2
1.0	1.0	1.0	1.0
0.8	0.8	0.8	0.8
0.6	0.6	0.6	0.6
0.4	0.4	0.4	0.4
0.2	0.2	0.2	0.2
0.0	0.0	0.0	0.0

As the grade reports become available, please circle your GPA in these columns.

_____

(My Name)

Progress Report on Achievement

My GPA first quarter: _____

My GPA goal for the end of the semester: _____

Classes

Reporting Times

1. _____

Estimate Actual Goal Actual Goal Actual Goal Actual

2. _____

Estimate Actual Goal Actual Goal Actual Goal Actual

3. _____

Estimate Actual Goal Actual Goal Actual Goal Actual

4. _____

Estimate Actual Goal Actual Goal Actual Goal Actual

5. _____

Estimate Actual Goal Actual Goal Actual Goal Actual

6. _____

Estimate Actual Goal Actual Goal Actual Goal Actual

7. _____

Estimate Actual Goal Actual Goal Actual Goal Actual

DECISION MAKING

Which would give me a GPA of . . .

_____ _____ _____ _____

As the grade reports become available, please circle your GPA in these columns.

4.0	4.0	4.0	4.0
3.8	3.8	3.8	3.8
3.6	3.6	3.6	3.6
3.4	3.4	3.4	3.4
3.2	3.2	3.2	3.2
3.0	3.0	3.0	3.0
2.8	2.8	2.8	2.8
2.6	2.6	2.6	2.6
2.4	2.4	2.4	2.4
2.2	2.2	2.2	2.2
2.0	2.0	2.0	2.0
1.8	1.8	1.8	1.8
1.6	1.6	1.6	1.6
1.4	1.4	1.4	1.4
1.2	1.2	1.2	1.2
1.0	1.0	1.0	1.0
0.8	0.8	0.8	0.8
0.6	0.6	0.6	0.6
0.4	0.4	0.4	0.4
0.2	0.2	0.2	0.2
0.0	0.0	0.0	0.0

_____
(My Name)

Time Management Review

Examples of two 24-hour time wheels appear on the next page. The first wheel is a weekend day wheel (either Saturday or Sunday). The second wheel is a weekday wheel (Monday through Friday). Before filling out the blank time wheels on the third page of this worksheet, think about and complete the items below.

1. You have developed to-do lists and talked with some of your teachers about plans for improving your grades in one or more of your classes. The decisions you have made may mean increasing the amount of time you spend doing homework.

2. Review your to-do lists (see Worksheet 84), and identify tasks that you plan to do in the next 7 days. Write these tasks below, and estimate the amount of time needed (in hours) to complete each task.

Tasks	Time to complete
_____	_____
_____	_____
_____	_____
_____	_____
_____	_____
_____	_____

3. Exchange workbooks with your partner. Look at the tasks and the amount of time estimated to complete each one. Give each other feedback on whether the tasks and time estimates are reasonable. Then support and encourage each other to work toward completing these tasks.

(continued)

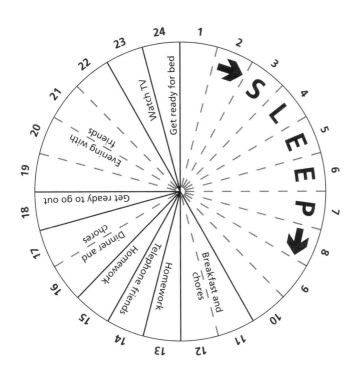

Weekend Wheel

(Saturday or Sunday)

ACTIVITY	TIME
Sleep	10
Breakfast, chores	2
Homework	1
Telephone friends	1
Homework	1
Dinner, chores	2
Get ready to go out	1
Evening with friends	4
Watch TV	1
Get ready for bed	1

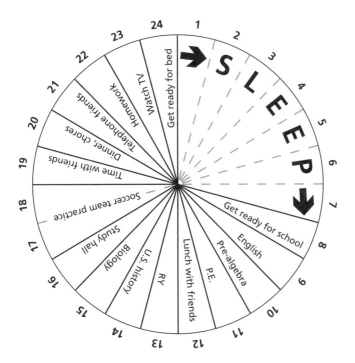

Weekday Wheel

(Monday through Friday)

ACTIVITY	TIME
Sleep	7
Get ready for school	1
School	8
Soccer practice	2
Time with friends	1
Dinner, chores	1
Telephone friends	1
Homework	1
Watch TV	1
Get ready for bed	1

DECISION MAKING

(continued)

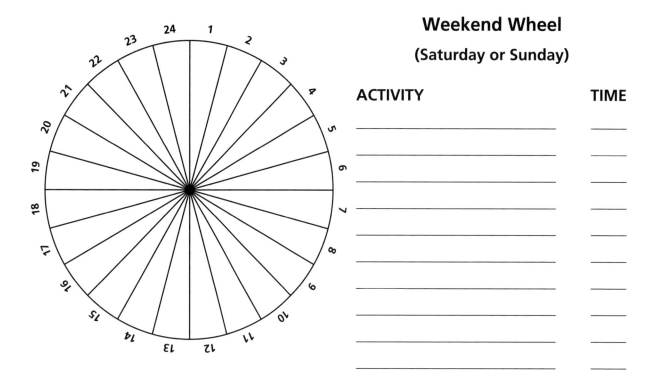

Weekend Wheel

(Saturday or Sunday)

ACTIVITY   TIME

_____   _____

_____   _____

_____   _____

_____   _____

_____   _____

_____   _____

_____   _____

_____   _____

_____   _____

_____   _____

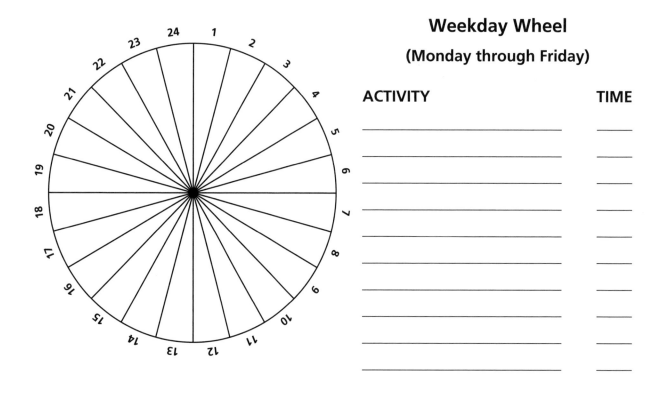

Weekday Wheel

(Monday through Friday)

ACTIVITY   TIME

_____   _____

_____   _____

_____   _____

_____   _____

_____   _____

_____   _____

_____   _____

_____   _____

_____   _____

_____   _____

CONTRACT TO PRACTICE

Time Management

1. What one block of time have you scheduled for the next 24 hours to do something that is important to you, but may be difficult to fit in? Write the name of this block of time below:

   _____

2. Discuss with your partner how you will manage your time in order to include your chosen activity. Then complete this sentence:

   I will fit in my activity by managing my time as follows:

   _____

   _____

   _____

   _____

3. Exchange workbooks with your partner and write a note of support and encouragement to accomplish the chosen activity.

   Note of support and encouragement from my partner:

Be prepared to follow up with your partner tomorrow to see if the activities he or she chose were accomplished.

Using STEPS to Improve Drug-Use Control

1. Flag this page with a self-stick note. Then turn to Worksheet 13, "Drug-Use and Non-Use Decisions."

2. Using colored pencils, mark where you currently are on your use and non-use history graph. Write in today's date.

3. Look at your graph and at your "Drug-Use Control Diary." Think about the decisions you made early in the semester about whether or not to use, and compare them to the decisions you are currently making. Write your opinion of how these decisions compare below.

_____

_____

_____

_____

4. Write examples of decisions you have made recently about whether or not to use drugs. Determine whether each decision was helpful or hurtful.

	Helpful	Hurtful
_____	❏	❏
_____	❏	❏
_____	❏	❏
_____	❏	❏

5. Work with the group to use STEPS to "re-decide" a hurtful drug-use decision and change it to a helpful drug-use control decision.

Sample Drug-Use Control Goal to Decrease Use

Your goal should be

DESIRABLE • SPECIFIC • ACHIEVABLE

Drug-Use Control Goal

My RY drug-use control goal for this semester is to . . .

Stay drug-free on weekdays and weeknights (Mondays through Thursdays). That includes cigarettes, marijuana, alcohol, and any other drug that I might be tempted to use.

Mini-Goals

My mini-goals for accomplishing this bigger goal are to . . .

- Stay drug-free before school (not even a cigarette).

- Stay drug-free between classes (not even a cigarette).

- Stay drug-free during lunch time.

- Use STEPS to stop and think through my decisions if I am distracted from my goal.

To-Do List

Things I will need to do to accomplish my mini-goals are to . . .

Tasks	Do by	✓ if Done
• Go straight to first period when I arrive at school.	Daily	_____
• Visit with friends in the hallways between classes.	Daily	_____
• Eat lunch on campus, or go to lunch with friends who don't use.	Daily	_____
• Bring lots of gum to school.	Daily	_____

DECISION MAKING

Sample Drug-Use Control Goal to Maintain Non-Drug Use

Your goal should be

DESIRABLE • SPECIFIC • ACHIEVABLE

Drug-Use Control Goal

My RY drug-use control goal for this semester is to . . .

Continue to stay drug-free while supporting my classmates as they set goals to decrease their use.

Mini-Goals

My mini-goals for accomplishing this bigger goal are to . . .

- Keep in mind my personal reasons for not using.

- Use STEPS to make decisions if I am distracted from my goal.

- Support my RY classmates every day as they work on their goals.

To-Do List

Things I will need to do to accomplish my mini-goals are to . . .

Tasks	Do by	✓ if Done
• Continue to do things with people who don't use.	Daily	_____
• Ask my RY classmates how I can support them in not using; get specifics of one helpful thing I can do or say.	Friday	_____
• Be respectful when I disagree with my RY classmates about their drug use.	Always	_____
• Plan fun drug-free weekend activity.	Friday	_____
• Invite _____ or _____ to lunch with me (classmates who are trying to stay drug free).	Wednesday	_____

My RY Drug-Use Control Goal, Mini-Goals, and To-Do List

Your goal should be

DESIRABLE • SPECIFIC • ACHIEVABLE

RY Drug-Use Control Goal for This Semester

Mini-Goals for RY Goal

- _____
- _____
- _____
- _____

DECISION MAKING

To-Do List

Tasks	Do by	✓ if Done
• _____	_____	_____
• _____	_____	_____
• _____	_____	_____
• _____	_____	_____
• _____	_____	_____
• _____	_____	_____

CONTRACT TO PRACTICE

Using STEPS to Improve Drug-Use Control

My **drug-use control goal** for the rest of the semester is to . . .

In the next 24 hours, I will work on the following **mini-goal** to improve my drug-use control:

A **barrier** that might get in my way would be . . .

Practice with your partner using STEPS to deal with your barrier.

◎ **Stop:** What will I say to myself to stop and think this through?

◎ **Think:** What are my options?

◎ **Evaluate:** Which options help me meet my goal? (Helpful) Which options lead me away from my goal? (Hurtful)

◎ **Perform:** What will I do? When? How?

◎ **Self-Praise:** How will I praise myself?

Be prepared to share with the group what happened when you used STEPS to improve your drug-use control.

Booster: What Can I Say?

1 Write one example of a situation where you might want to talk to someone about his or her drug use.

_____

_____

_____

_____

_____

_____

2 Think about and then write one way you might bring up the subject with this person (an opening line).

_____

_____

_____

_____

_____

3 What constructive feedback, observations, information, or advice would you want to share with this person?

_____

_____

_____

_____

_____

Develop two role plays demonstrating what you might say to someone if you were worried about his or her drug use. Be prepared to share your role plays with the group.

DECISION MAKING

Booster: Are You Taking STEPS?

Directions: Use this evaluation sheet to think about how you made a recent drug-use decision and whether or not you want or need to change your style of decision making.

What Was Your Decision?

_____

_____

✓ **Check off any STEPS you took to make your decision.**

_____   Before acting, I **STOPPED** and considered the possible consequences of my decision.

_____   I **THOUGHT** about other options I might have.

_____   I **EVALUATED** which options might be helpful and which might be hurtful.

_____   I **PERFORMED** or took action on my decision.

_____   I used **SELF-PRAISE** for making a helpful decision.

Did your decision get you want you wanted?   ❏ YES   ❏ NO

What decision-making style did you use? (See Worksheet 65.)

_____

_____

What, if anything, would you change about how you made this decision?

_____

_____

_____

CONTRACT TO PRACTICE

Taking STEPS

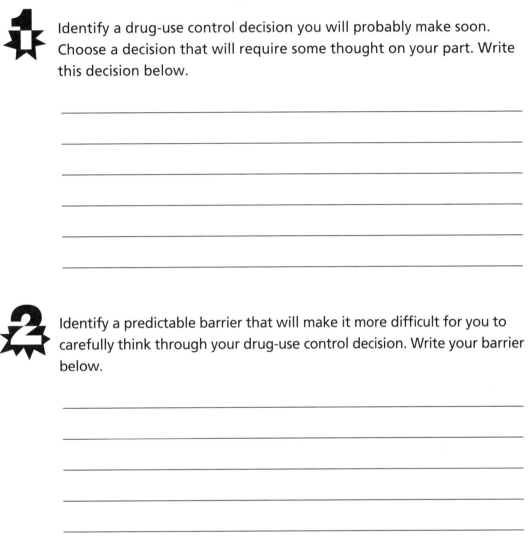

1 Identify a drug-use control decision you will probably make soon. Choose a decision that will require some thought on your part. Write this decision below.

_____

_____

_____

_____

_____

_____

2 Identify a predictable barrier that will make it more difficult for you to carefully think through your drug-use control decision. Write your barrier below.

_____

_____

_____

_____

_____

_____

 3 Decide how you will use STEPS to deal with your barrier and stick to your drug-use control goal.

(continued)

CONTRACT TO PRACTICE

4 Work with a partner to develop two role plays—one for each of you—in which you practice using STEPS to make your drug-use control decision.

Stop: What will you say to yourself to stop and think this through?

_____

_____

_____

Think: What are my options?

_____

_____

_____

Evaluate: Which options are helpful? Which are hurtful?

_____

_____

_____

Perform: What will you do?

_____

_____

_____

Self-Praise: How will you praise yourself?

_____

_____

_____

Be prepared to share your role plays with the group.

CES-D* Mood Questionnaire

Student's Name_____ Course/Instructor_____

Circle the number for each statement that best describes how often you felt this way *during the past week.* A few of the numbers for your response are listed in reverse order. Simply choose the number in the column that best describes your experience. **This questionnaire is confidential.** You will not be asked to share the results with the group.

During the Past Week	Rarely or None of the Time (less than 1 day)	Some or a Little of the Time (1–2 days)	Occasionally or a Moderate Amount of Time (3–4 days)	Most or All of the Time (5–7 days)
1. I was bothered by things that usually don't bother me.	0	1	2	3
2. I didn't feel like eating; my appetite was poor.	0	1	2	3
3. I felt that I couldn't shake off the blues, even with help from my family or friends.	0	1	2	3
4. I felt that I was just as good as other people.	3	2	1	0
5. I had trouble keeping my mind on what I was doing.	0	1	2	3
6. I felt depressed.	0	1	2	3
7. I felt that everything I did was an effort.	0	1	2	3
8. I felt hopeful about the future.	3	2	1	0
9. I thought my life had been a failure.	0	1	2	3
10. I felt fearful.	0	1	2	3

*Center for Epidemiologic Studies-Depression Scale, National Institute of Mental Health.

(continued)

DECISION MAKING

CES-D Mood Questionnaire

During the Past Week	Rarely or None of the Time (less than 1 day)	Some or a Little of the Time (1–2 days)	Occasionally or a Moderate Amount of Time (3–4 days)	Most or All of the Time (5–7 days)
11. My sleep was restless.	0	1	2	3
12. I was happy.	3	2	1	0
13. I talked less than usual.	0	1	2	3
14. I felt lonely.	0	1	2	3
15. People were unfriendly.	0	1	2	3
16. I enjoyed life.	3	2	1	0
17. I had crying spells.	0	1	2	3
18. I felt sad.	0	1	2	3
19. I felt that people disliked me.	0	1	2	3
20. I could not "get going."	0	1	2	3

Scoring

Add up all of the numbers you have circled. If you have circled more than one number for a statement, add only the largest number to your score.

The numbers for your responses on four of the statements (numbers 4, 8, 12, and 16) are listed in reverse order. This has been done on purpose. Your score will be correct if you simply add up all the numbers you have circled.

Total Score: _____

Working With Your CES-D Score

The average teen score is about 17.

Low scores are from 0 to 23.

Medium scores are from 24 to 32.

High scores are from 33 to 60.

Date _____   Your CES-D Score _____

1. Were you surprised by your score? If so, in what way? If not, why not?

2. Use the questions in the CES-D questionnaire to identify which feelings you would like to work on changing.

3. Moods go up and moods go down. In your experience:

    • My mood tends to go up when . . .

    • My mood tends to go down when . . .

For the next 24 hours, observe your mood swings. Be prepared to report back to the group at the next class on what contributed to changes in your mood.

DECISION MAKING

Sample Mood Management Goal, Mini-Goals, and To-Do List

Your goal should be

DESIRABLE • SPECIFIC • ACHIEVABLE

RY Mood Management Goal for This Semester

Decrease the amount of depression I'm feeling.

Mini-Goals for RY Goal

- Identify fun activities I could do that would decrease my depression.

- Identify the situations that usually trigger my depression.

- Remember to use the skills we've learned in RY to decrease my depression.

To-Do List

Tasks	Do by	✓ if Done
• Make a list of fun activities I could do when I'm starting to feel depressed.	Today	_____
• Make a list of situations that typically trigger my depression.	Today	_____
• Develop a list of strategies to deal with these situations.	Today	_____
• Share my list of situations that trigger my depression with the RY group and ask for their suggestions.	Today	_____
• Choose one strategy at a time, and practice using it so I'm comfortable with it.	This Week	_____
• Monitor my use of these strategies to determine how effective they are.	This Week	_____

Mood Management Goal, Mini-Goals, and To-Do List

Your goal should be

DESIRABLE • SPECIFIC • ACHIEVABLE

RY Mood Management Goal for This Semester

- _____

Mini-Goals for RY Goal

- _____
- _____
- _____
- _____

To-Do List

Tasks	Do by	✓ if Done
• _____	_____	_____
• _____	_____	_____
• _____	_____	_____
• _____	_____	_____
• _____	_____	_____
• _____	_____	_____

DECISION MAKING

CONTRACT TO PRACTICE

Improving Moods

In the next 24 hours, I will make time for the following healthy fun activity:

I will also work on the following mini-goal to improve my ability to manage my moods:

Note of support and encouragement from my partner on my effort to improve my moods:

Booster: Our Moods Banner

Work in small groups of two or three to produce an artistic "masterpiece" that presents a visual image of moods—good moods, bad moods, moods spiraling up, and moods spiraling down!

Your masterpiece can include words, drawings, colors, and stickers—it can include whatever socially acceptable images you want to include.

Be prepared to tell the group about your work of art before adding it to our group's Moods Banner.

DECISION MAKING

Booster: Recognition of Improvement

Directions: Use the scale below to estimate how you are doing in each of the areas listed. In the first column, write in the number that you feel represents where you were at the beginning of RY. In the second column, write in the number that summarizes how you are currently doing.

Scale: 1   →   2   →   3   →   4   →   5

Doing poorly   **Doing okay**   **Doing great**

	Where I Was _____ (Date)	**Where I Am Now** _____ (Date)
GOAL AREA		
School attendance	_____	_____
School achievement	_____	_____
Likelihood of dropping out	_____	_____
Drug use	_____	_____
Smoking	_____	_____
Anger or depression	_____	_____
Relationships with teachers	_____	_____
Relationships with friends	_____	_____
Relationships at home	_____	_____

Certificate of Award

May it be known by all who read this that a Certificate of Award has been presented to

for Outstanding Achievement and Accomplishment in

Reconnecting Youth

Signed

Presented this _____ Day of _____

DECISION MAKING

Personal Control

Body Language

A hundred times a day, you worry: What am I going to do?

You know he'll come around again, looking for a fight. You just don't know when. Days go by, and still you worry.

You don't want to fight. You avoid him, but it's no good. He'll find you and call you a liar or worse. He's made a game out of making you mad, and you lose every time. You can't sleep. You can't eat. What can you do?

You hear a voice like an echo in your head. "Hey, you! Are you listening to me?" You turn on the radio, but the voice is still there. You change radio stations, hoping it will go away, but there it is again, slow and stubborn. "Hellooo. Anyone home? I—am— talking—to—you."

What talk? Who's talking? You put the Big Worry aside and listen to your body language: Your legs are shaking, your stomach aches, and you can hardly breathe.

All of a sudden, you can hear what your body's saying: "Give me a break! I need to sleep, and I need to eat. Being afraid he'll fight you isn't the only thing to worry about. How about me?"

Then you understand: The kid has made a place in your head where he can worry you day and night until you find a way to make him quit. He's controlling my life, you think. He's controlling me! How do I get back in control?

The answer? Turn the page.

This part of Reconnecting Youth will help you understand how you react to problems and give you new ways of taking control of what you think and do.

PERSONAL CONTROL

Personal Control: An Overview

Definition: Personal control means coping successfully with stress.

PATHWAYS TO PERSONAL CONTROL VERSUS STRESS

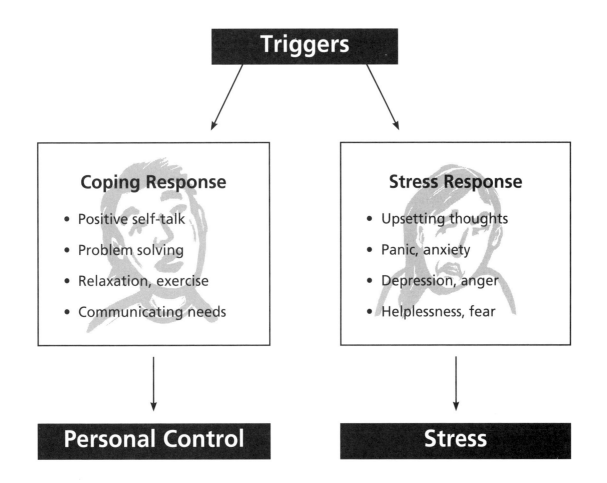

Triggers

Coping Response

- Positive self-talk
- Problem solving
- Relaxation, exercise
- Communicating needs

Stress Response

- Upsetting thoughts
- Panic, anxiety
- Depression, anger
- Helplessness, fear

Personal Control

Stress

WHY PRACTICE PERSONAL CONTROL?

- ◎ Gives you **control** of your thoughts and actions
- ◎ Opens up **helpful** options
- ◎ Makes you feel **healthy,** physically and emotionally
- ◎ Increases your **self-confidence**
- ◎ Earns you **respect** from others

PERSONAL CONTROL

Stress Triggers

Conflicts With People

- Friends
- Family
- Teachers
- Bosses, co-workers

Inner Conflicts

- How I look, act
- What I'm accomplishing
- My future

Changes

- Loss of relative, friend
- Moving
- New job
- New school

Situations

- Money worries
- Family, friend in trouble
- Learning, skill problems

What triggers stress me in my life?

⚡ _____

⚡ _____

⚡ _____

⚡ _____

⚡ _____

Reconnecting Youth © 2004 Solution Tree

Feeling Stressed Out

Directions: Sketch a picture of yourself feeling stressed out. Add words to your picture that describe your physical reactions, thoughts, and feelings when you are stressed.

PERSONAL CONTROL

CONTRACT TO PRACTICE

Observing Trigger Situations

My three most common or troublesome stress triggers are . . .

1. _____
   _____

2. _____
   _____

3. _____
   _____

Between now and our next session, keep track of those situations that trigger stress for you. Be prepared to share your observations with the group.

Situations

- _____

- _____

- _____

- _____

- _____

- _____

- _____

- _____

- _____

Stressful Events Scale for Adolescents

This list of problems or stressful events contains a range of things that people your age sometimes experience. As you look at each one, put a checkmark in Column 1 if you have **ever** experienced it. Think about how much each problem or stressful event you checked has been bothering you during the last 2 weeks, including today. Then select a number from the scale below and write it in Column 2.

Scale: 0　　1　　2　　3　　4　　5　　6

Not at all　　A little　　Moderately　　Very much

	1. Ever Experienced?	2. Effect Last 2 Weeks
1. Feeling depressed	_____	_____
2. Feeling I didn't matter	_____	_____
3. Having daily hassles pile up	_____	_____
4. Conflict with brother/sister	_____	_____
5. Conflict with girlfriend/boyfriend	_____	_____
6. Breakup with girlfriend/boyfriend	_____	_____
7. Family member sick	_____	_____
8. Conflict among family members	_____	_____
9. Problems in school	_____	_____
10. Conflict with friends	_____	_____
11. Feeling like I had no friends	_____	_____
12. My job interferes with getting schoolwork done	_____	_____
13. Problems at work	_____	_____
14. Feeling I have too many responsibilities in my life	_____	_____
15. Bothered by not having the money to buy or do the things I want	_____	_____
16. Fear of pregnancy/getting someone pregnant	_____	_____
17. Keeping or having a relationship with a girlfriend/boyfriend	_____	_____
18. Significant weight gain or loss (without dieting) (more than 10% of body weight)	_____	_____

PERSONAL CONTROL

(continued)

Stressful Events Scale for Adolescents (continued)

Scale: 0   1   2   3   4   5   6

Not at all   **A little**   **Moderately**   **Very much**

		1. EVER EXPERIENCED?	2. EFFECT LAST 2 WEEKS
19.	Close friend is very depressed	_____	_____
20.	Family member is very depressed	_____	_____
21.	Parent quit or lost job	_____	_____
22.	Death of a friend or family member	_____	_____
23.	Parental violence toward family member	_____	_____
24.	Pregnancy/abortion or getting someone pregnant	_____	_____
25.	Sexual abuse or rape	_____	_____
26.	Dropping out of school	_____	_____
27.	Sexually transmitted disease	_____	_____
28.	Thoughts of being gay or lesbian	_____	_____
29.	Drug and/or alcohol abuse	_____	_____
30.	Major health problem or chronic illness	_____	_____

Type:_____

Is there anything not included on this list that you would add? If yes, what has happened? State the problem, put a checkmark in Column 1, and rate the frequency of the problem in Column 2.

31. Type:_____   _____   _____

Of all the items you checked, which three are affecting you the most?

Item
Number   Event

32. _____   _____

33. _____   _____

34. _____   _____

(continued)

Stressful Events Scale for Adolescents (continued)

Total Scores

Count all checks in Column 1 ("Ever experienced?") and record the number below.

1. Total number of stressors experienced: _____

   Compute stress level by adding all numbers greater than 0 in Column 2 and dividing by total number of stressors checked in Column 1.

2. Level of stress: _____) _____ = _____

                                   Sum of   Sum of
                                   Column 2   Column 1

3. Interpreting score:

   After you have determined your stress level, find the number on the stress scale below to get a sense of how you are being affected by stress.

Scale: 0   1   2   3   4   5   6
        Not at all   **A little**   **Moderately** **Very much**

PERSONAL CONTROL

Excerpted with permission from the Measure of Adolescent Potential for Suicide developed by Leona L. Eggert, Ph.D., R.N.; Elaine A. Thompson, Ph.D., R.N.; Jerald R. Herting, Ph.D.; and Christine Seyl, M.N., R.N., and published in *Suicide and Life-Threatening Behavior (24)*4, January 1, 1994: 359–381.

Booster: My Stress Thermometer

Directions: Think about how much stress you're experiencing in your life at this time. If you were to take your stress "temperature," what would it be? Are you stressed to the maximum? Would you call that an "overload" or "dangerous"? Is your stress level just about right—not too much stress, but enough stress to keep life interesting? Or do you have too little stress in your life? Is there nothing happening for you right now? How would you measure your level of stress? **Draw an arrow at the correct level to measure your stress.**

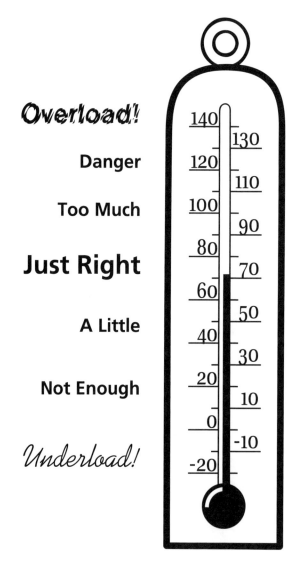

Overload!

Danger

Too Much

Just Right

A Little

Not Enough

Underload!

Adapted with permission from *The Stress Connection* (1981), National 4-H Council, 7100 Connecticut Avenue, Chevy Chase, MD 20815.

CONTRACT TO PRACTICE

Tracking Your Reactions to Stress

Between now and our next class, when a situation triggers stress for you, keep track of your reactions to the stress. What kinds of physical and/or emotional responses do you experience when you are stressed?

Situation

Responses

1. _____

- _____
- _____
- _____
- _____

2. _____

- _____
- _____
- _____
- _____

3. _____

- _____
- _____
- _____
- _____

4. _____

- _____
- _____
- _____
- _____

5. _____

- _____
- _____
- _____
- _____

Stress Reactions

Directions: Put a dot next to the physical symptoms of stress that you've experienced. At the bottom of the page, put checks before things that you do when stressed.

PHYSICAL SYMPTOMS I HAVE WHEN STRESSED

____ Skin problems

____ Headaches

____ Dizziness

____ Teeth grinding

____ Tight neck/shoulders

____ Dry mouth/throat

____ Shortness of breath

____ Nail biting

____ Rapid heartbeat

____ Backaches

____ Stomach upset/nausea

____ Legs shaky or tight

____ Diarrhea/constipation

____ Foot/finger tapping

____ Hands/feet cold or sweaty

THINGS I DO WHEN STRESSED

____Cry

____Become exhausted

____Become aggressive

____Become bored

____Eat too much

____Become depressed

____Increase smoking

____Sleep too much

____Become distracted

____Eat too little

____Become nervous

____Misuse drugs/alcohol

____Sleep too little

____Withdraw from people

____Other:_____

Sample Stress Triggers, Reactions, and Their Effects on My Life

Directions: Think about the three most common or troublesome stressors you are experiencing right now in your life. Write these three under "Triggers" on the chart below. Then identify the reactions you experience to these stressors and the effects these stressors and your reactions have on your life.

Triggers (What is the source of my stress?)	Reactions (What are my physical reactions, thoughts, feelings?)	Effects (What are the effects on my life?)
1. F grade on test	• Angry • Discouraged • Headache, Stomachache	• Skipped my next class • Drank way too much alcohol • Won't do homework tonight
2. Fight with best friend	• Angry, felt hurt • Depressed • Diarrhea	• Won't talk to my friend • Skipped class; swore and cried • Went home sick
3. Grounded because of drinking at school	• Angry at parents, teacher, and principal • Nausea, diarrhea	• Won't talk to my parents • Suspended for 5 days • Felt awful

PERSONAL CONTROL

Stress Triggers, Reactions, and Their Effects on My Life

Directions: Think about the three most common or troublesome stressors you are experiencing right now in your life. Write these three under "Triggers" on the chart below. Then identify the reactions you experience to these stressors and the effects these stressors and your reactions have on your life.

Triggers (What is the source of my stress?)	Reactions (What are my physical reactions, thoughts, feelings?)	Effects (What are the effects on my life?)
1. _____	_____ _____ _____	_____ _____ _____
2. _____	_____ _____ _____	_____ _____ _____
3. _____	_____ _____ _____	_____ _____ _____

CONTRACT TO PRACTICE

Responding to Stress

1. In general, how do you usually respond to stress? Identify any patterns in your response to stressful situations.

    _____

    _____

    _____

    _____

    _____

    _____

2. Select one stress trigger you are likely to experience before our group meets again. Write this trigger below.

    _____

    _____

    _____

    _____

    _____

    _____

3. Monitor your reaction to this trigger. Be prepared to share with the group what your response or reaction was and how much your response interfered with your life. Be prepared to give your response a rating from 1 (did not interfere at all) to 10 (interfered a great deal).

Booster: Your Piece of the Pie (Sample)

Life Event:

My parents are fighting constantly. They yell and scream and are threatening to get a divorce.

I am personally responsible for . . .

when I do something wrong that adds to their stress and their fighting (for example, come home late, get caught using drugs, skip school, and get suspended).

I am not responsible for . . .

how they deal with their stress, my father being unfaithful to my mother, my mother refusing to cook anymore for my father, and so on. They have to solve the problems in their relationship.

I am making these specific choices:

1. I will try to get my act together and quit getting into so much trouble—for my future.

2. I will tell them that I don't want them trying to make me take sides.

3. I will also tell them that it's very hard to be around them when they are yelling and screaming. I will ask them to try to be a little more gentle and a little more quiet in their disagreements.

4. I will make arrangements to go to the library to do my homework.

Booster: Your Piece of the Pie

Life Event:

_____

_____

I am personally responsible for . . .

_____

_____

I am not responsible for . . .

_____

_____

I am making these specific choices:

1. _____

2. _____

3. _____

4. _____

PERSONAL CONTROL

CONTRACT TO PRACTICE

Sample Using STEPS to Reduce Stress

Identify a stressful situation that is likely to occur in the next 24 hours. Practice with your partner doing a QR and then using STEPS to handle the situation. Be prepared to share how it went at our next group.

Briefly describe the situation:

Got back a paper with a really low grade on it.

STOP *What will I say to myself to slow down so I can think this through?*

STOP! Take a deep breath. Do a QR!

THINK *SNAP out bad thoughts! ZAP in positive thoughts!*

SNAP!	**ZAP!**
1. I'll always fail, so why try?	1. Guess I'd better study harder.
2. That's the last time I turn in a paper!	2. I'll start earlier on my next paper.
3. The teacher is really unfair!	3. I wonder if my teacher will help me?
4. I'm skipping the rest of the day!	4. I need to calm down!

EVALUATE *What's my piece of the pie? Which options are healthy?*

HEALTHY OPTIONS:

- Calm down
- Begin my next paper now
- Ask teacher for some help
- Study harder

PERFORM *What will I do? When? How?*

I will start right now by calming down. Do I need to do another QR? Then I will ask the teacher if I can see her today after school to discuss what went wrong on my paper and get some help before I start my next paper.

SELF-PRAISE *How will I praise myself?*

Good decision. I didn't make a bad situation worse by blowing up!

CONTRACT TO PRACTICE

Using STEPS to Reduce Stress

Identify a stressful situation that is likely to occur in the next 24 hours. Practice with your partner doing a QR and then using STEPS to handle the situation. Be prepared to share how it went at our next group.

Briefly describe the situation:

_____

_____

STOP *What will I do and say to myself to slow down and think this through?*
Do a QR and say the following to myself:

_____

_____

THINK *SNAP out bad thoughts! ZAP in positive thoughts!*

SNAP!

1. _____
2. _____
3. _____
4. _____

ZAP!

1. _____
2. _____
3. _____
4. _____

EVALUATE *What's my piece of the pie? Which options are healthy?*

_____

_____

PERFORM *What will I do? When? How?*

_____

_____

SELF-PRAISE *How will I praise myself?*

_____

_____

Using STEPS to Reduce Stress Helper Worksheet

After your partner has identified a stressful situation, use this worksheet to help your partner practice using STEPS.

Ask your partner to briefly describe the situation.

GUIDE YOUR PARTNER THROUGH THE STEPS PROCESS.

STOP Have your partner practice doing a QR. (Remind your partner to **stop**, take a deep breath, and do a quieting response as soon as the stressful situation occurs.)

THINK What negative thoughts need to be SNAPPED out? What positive thoughts should be ZAPPED in? Encourage your partner to identify three or more negative thoughts that typically occur. Replace these with positive thoughts.

EVALUATE Encourage your partner to identify a number of healthy alternative ways to respond to the stressful situation. Help your partner identify new or different options.

PERFORM Ask your partner to select an option that deals with the situation appropriately while also reducing the stressful response. What will your partner do? When? How?

SELF-PRAISE Praise your partner. Be specific about what you liked about how the stressful situation was handled. If appropriate, give encouragement or advice. Ask your partner to also praise him- or herself!

What Qualities Does a Good Support Person Have?

Work together with a partner to identify and discuss the qualities that a good support person has. Think about examples of what a support person does (for example, a support person listens carefully) and what a support person says (for example, a support person gives good advice).

List below the qualities that you think a good support person has.

1 _____

2 _____

3 _____

4 _____

5 _____

6 _____

PERSONAL CONTROL

Sample Building a Support Network

Your support network can help you control your level of stress.

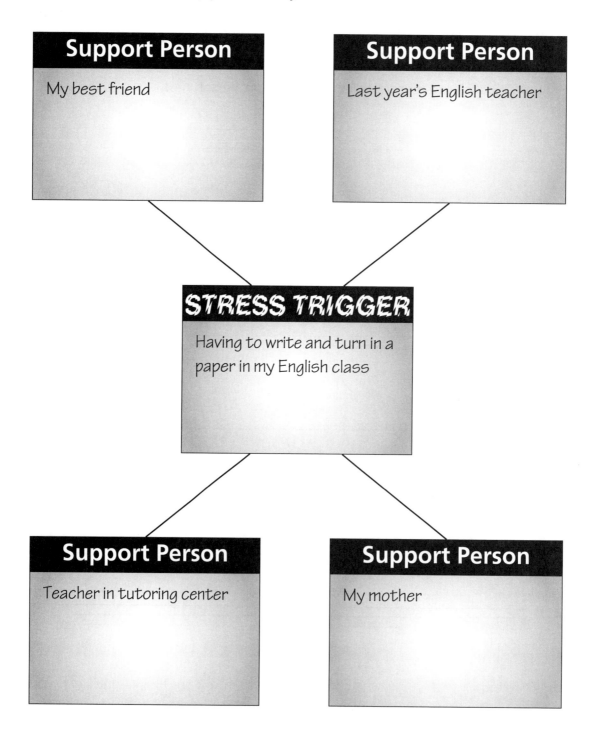

Support Person

My best friend

Support Person

Last year's English teacher

STRESS TRIGGER

Having to write and turn in a paper in my English class

Support Person

Teacher in tutoring center

Support Person

My mother

Building a Support Network

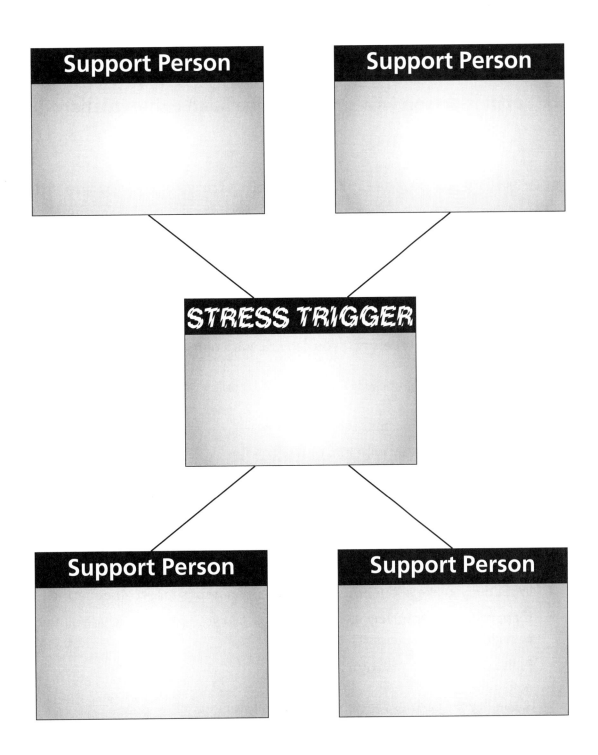

Support Person

Support Person

STRESS TRIGGER

Support Person

Support Person

PERSONAL CONTROL

Reconnecting Youth © 2004 Solution Tree

Practice Asking for Support

Think of a stressful situation that you often experience. Who would be a good support person to help you handle the situation?

A stressful situation that occurs often:

_____

A good support person who could help me handle the situation:

_____

Together with your partner, practice asking for support for the situation you identified above.

1. YOU: Briefly describe the stressful situation, and tell your partner how to be your support person. (Describe a few of the support person's qualities to help your partner know how to respond as your support person.)

2. YOU: Ask your support person if you can talk with him or her.

3. PARTNER: Respond that now is an okay time to talk.

4. YOU: Briefly tell your partner the following:
   - Why you need to talk with him or her
   - What you need to talk about
   - What you would like from him or her

5. PARTNER (no longer in role as support person): Respond with feedback on your partner's performance:
   - What did you like about how your partner asked for support? (be specific)
   - If appropriate, sensitively give suggestions. Did your partner include all the parts of asking for support?
   - Praise and build confidence.

6. YOU: thank your partner for responding and listening.

Reverse roles and repeat steps 1–5 above.

CONTRACT TO PRACTICE

Asking for Support

Select one person you will talk to in the next week to request his or her help in handling a stressful situation.

What stressful situation will I seek help for?

_____

_____

_____

_____

Who will I talk to?

_____

_____

_____

When will I talk to this person?

_____

_____

_____

Remember: Your support network
can help you control your level of stress.

Sample Fun Activity Log

1. Write 10 or more activities you enjoy in the first column.
2. In the next four columns, put a checkmark under any of the following codes that apply to the activities:
   S = I do this with someone else. $ = This costs money.   HH = This is a health hazard.   E = This involves physical exercise.
3. At the end of each day, check off the activities you have done in the column for that day and add up the total.
4. At the same time each day, rate your mood using the 10-point scale.

Fun Activities

		S	$	HH	E	Sa	Su	M	T	W	Th	F
1.	Snowboarding	✓	✓	✓	✓	✓	—	—	—	—	—	—
2.	Walk my dog	—	—	✓	✓	—	✓	✓	✓	✓	✓	✓
3.	Watch TV	✓	—	—	—	—	✓	✓	✓	✓	✓	✓
4.	Skateboarding	✓	—	✓	✓	✓	✓	✓	✓	✓	✓	✓
5.	Talk on the telephone	✓	✓	—	—	✓	✓	✓	—	—	✓	✓
6.	Rent, watch movies	✓	✓	—	—	✓	✓	—	✓	—	—	✓
7.	Go to the mall	✓	✓	—	—	—	—	—	—	—	—	—
8.	Listen to music	—	—	—	—	✓	✓	✓	✓	✓	✓	✓
9.	Read magazines	—	—	—	—	—	—	—	—	—	—	—
10.	Hang out with my friends	✓	—	—	—	✓	✓	✓	✓	✓	✓	✓
11.	Shoot hoops	—	—	—	—	—	✓	—	—	—	—	—
12.												

Add up the number of fun activities you did each day.

Sa	Su	M	T	W	Th	F
3	8	5	6	6	6	6

Rate your mood each day, using the 10-point scale below.

Sa	Su	M	T	W	Th	F
10	9	4	6	6	7	9

Scale:	1	2	3	4	5	6	7	8	9	10
	Very Sad				Normal Mood					Very Happy

Fun Activity Log

1. Write 10 or more activities you enjoy in the first column.
2. In the next four columns, put a checkmark under any of the following codes that apply to the activities:

   S = I do this with someone else.　　$ = This costs money.　　HH = This is a health hazard.　　E = This involves physical exercise.
3. At the end of each day, check off the activities you have done in the column for that day and add up the total.
4. At the same time each day, rate your mood using the 10-point scale.

Fun Activities

Fun Activities	S	$	HH	E	Sa	Su	M	T	W	Th	F
1.											
2.											
3.											
4.											
5.											
6.											
7.											
8.											
9.											
10.											
11.											
12.											
Add up the number of fun activities you did each day.					☐	☐	☐	☐	☐	☐	☐
Rate your mood each day, using the 10-point scale below.					☐	☐	☐	☐	☐	☐	☐

Scale:	1	2	3	4	5	6	7	8	9	10
	Very Sad				Normal Mood					Very Happy

PERSONAL CONTROL

Sample Progress Report on Achievement

My GPA first quarter: 1.5
My GPA goal for the end of the semester: 2.0 or higher

Classes   Reporting Times

	Time 1	Time 2	Time 3	Time 4
1. English	D Estimate Actual	C | D+ Goal Actual	C Goal Actual	Goal Actual
2. Pre-algebra	F Estimate Actual	D | D Goal Actual	C Goal Actual	Goal Actual
3. P.E.	A Estimate Actual	A | A Goal Actual	A Goal Actual	Goal Actual
4. RY	B Estimate Actual	A | B+ Goal Actual	A Goal Actual	Goal Actual
5. U.S. history	D Estimate Actual	C | D+ Goal Actual	C Goal Actual	Goal Actual
6. Biology	F Estimate Actual	D | D Goal Actual	C Goal Actual	Goal Actual
7. Study hall	N Estimate Actual	P | P Goal Actual	P Goal Actual	Goal Actual

Which would give me a GPA of . . .   1.5   (2.3) 1.8   (2.6)   _____

As the grade reports become available, please circle your GPA in these columns.

4.0	4.0	4.0	4.0
3.8	3.8	3.8	3.8
3.6	3.6	3.6	3.6
3.4	3.4	3.4	3.4
3.2	3.2	3.2	3.2
3.0	3.0	3.0	3.0
2.8	2.8	2.8	2.8
2.6	2.6	2.6	2.6
2.4	2.4	2.4	2.4
2.2	2.2	2.2	2.2
2.0	2.0	2.0	2.0
1.8	(1.8)	1.8	1.8
(1.6)	1.6	1.6	1.6
1.4	1.4	1.4	1.4
1.2	1.2	1.2	1.2
1.0	1.0	1.0	1.0
0.8	0.8	0.8	0.8
0.6	0.6	0.6	0.6
0.4	0.4	0.4	0.4
0.2	0.2	0.2	0.2
0.0	0.0	0.0	0.0

_____
(My Name)

Progress Report on Achievement

My GPA first quarter: _____

My GPA goal for the end of the semester: _____

Classes

Reporting Times

	Time 1	Time 2	Time 3	Time 4
1. _____	Estimate Actual	Goal Actual	Goal Actual	Goal Actual
2. _____	Estimate Actual	Goal Actual	Goal Actual	Goal Actual
3. _____	Estimate Actual	Goal Actual	Goal Actual	Goal Actual
4. _____	Estimate Actual	Goal Actual	Goal Actual	Goal Actual
5. _____	Estimate Actual	Goal Actual	Goal Actual	Goal Actual
6. _____	Estimate Actual	Goal Actual	Goal Actual	Goal Actual
7. _____	Estimate Actual	Goal Actual	Goal Actual	Goal Actual

Which would give me a GPA of . . .

_____ _____ _____ _____

As the grade reports become available, please circle your GPA in these columns.

4.0	4.0	4.0	4.0
3.8	3.8	3.8	3.8
3.6	3.6	3.6	3.6
3.4	3.4	3.4	3.4
3.2	3.2	3.2	3.2
3.0	3.0	3.0	3.0
2.8	2.8	2.8	2.8
2.6	2.6	2.6	2.6
2.4	2.4	2.4	2.4
2.2	2.2	2.2	2.2
2.0	2.0	2.0	2.0
1.8	1.8	1.8	1.8
1.6	1.6	1.6	1.6
1.4	1.4	1.4	1.4
1.2	1.2	1.2	1.2
1.0	1.0	1.0	1.0
0.8	0.8	0.8	0.8
0.6	0.6	0.6	0.6
0.4	0.4	0.4	0.4
0.2	0.2	0.2	0.2
0.0	0.0	0.0	0.0

_____
(My Name)

PERSONAL CONTROL

CONTRACT TO PRACTICE

Improving School Achievement

1. One class where I should, and would like to, improve my grade or attitude is . . .

   _____

2. What am I going to work on improving?

   • _____

   • _____

   • _____

3. What is one barrier that might make it difficult for me to improve?

   _____

4. What strategy will I use to overcome this barrier?

   _____

   _____

   Practice using this strategy with your partner.

5. Be prepared to report back during our next class on your progress and to give yourself a grade on your effort to improve in this class.

Handling School— Before and After

Draw a picture of yourself as you handled school at **the beginning of the semester**. Your picture can include drawings, words, colors—whatever you would like to include.

Now, draw a picture of how you are **currently** handling school.

Be prepared to share your pictures with the group and to talk about the differences, if any, between the two pictures.

PERSONAL CONTROL

The Tools I Use to Help Me Improve My Achievement

Listed below are the various tools you have been using to help you improve your school achievement. Think about each tool and decide how useful it has been in helping you improve your achievement. Rate the tool, and then write comments on how it has helped you improve your school achievement.

Rating from 1–5 (1 = Not Helpful, 5 = Helpful)   **Score**

Comment on how the tool has helped—or could help—you.

1. Weekly Attendance Chart
My comments about this tool:

_____   _____

_____

2. School Smarts Checklist
My comments about this tool:

_____   _____

_____

3. Removing Barriers to Success
My comments about this tool:

_____   _____

_____

4. How Can You Improve Your Grade?
My comments about this tool:

_____   _____

_____

5. Progress Report on Achievement
My comments about this tool:

_____   _____

_____

Sample Getting Support to Improve Achievement

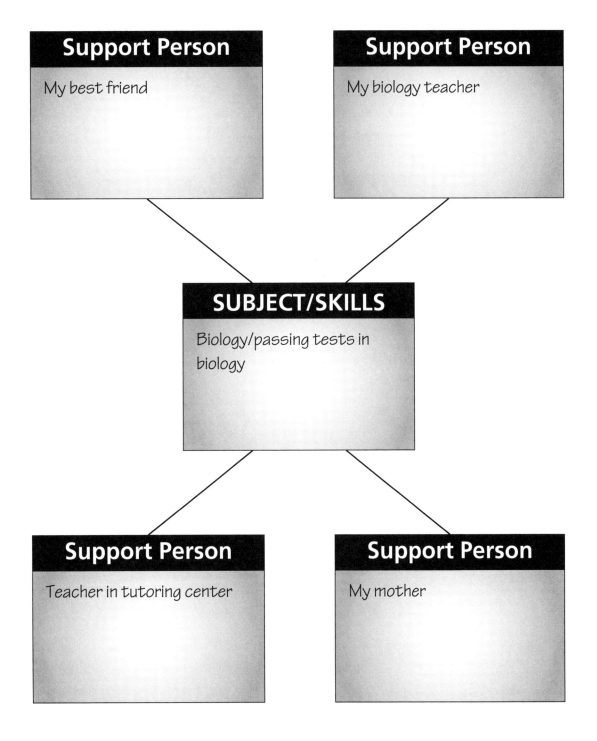

Support Person

My best friend

Support Person

My biology teacher

SUBJECT/SKILLS

Biology/passing tests in biology

Support Person

Teacher in tutoring center

Support Person

My mother

PERSONAL CONTROL

Getting Support to Improve Achievement

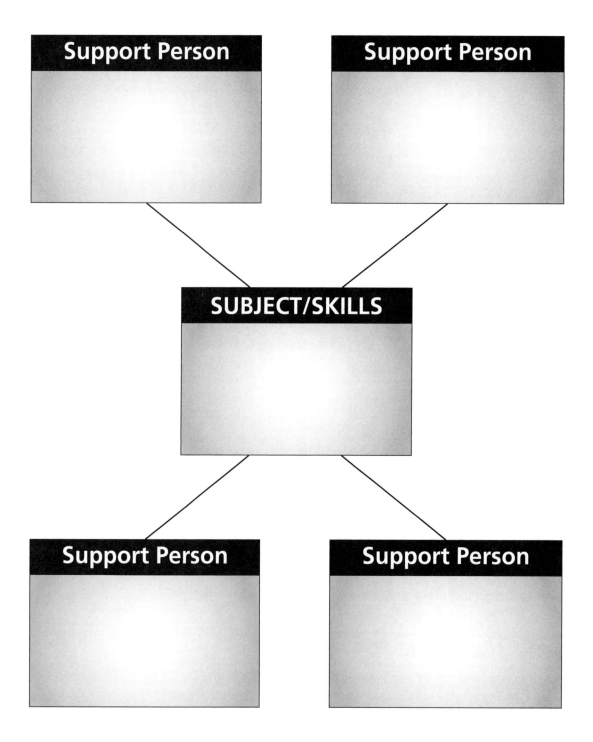

CONTRACT TO PRACTICE

Asking for Support

Think about your support network and select one person you will talk to in the next 24 hours to request his or her help in understanding a subject or improving one or more skills.

What subject or skills do I need to improve?

_____

_____

_____

Who will I talk to in the next 24 hours?

_____

_____

_____

What specific request for help will I make?

_____

_____

_____

If you have already received support from your support network, who would you thank for their support?

_____

_____

_____

Remember: Your support network can help you improve your school achievement.

Symptoms of Slips or Relapse

Put a check beside relapse symptoms you have experienced or may experience. Add any other symptoms you have noticed in yourself.

_____ 1. Saying that problems are smaller than they really are

_____ 2. Setting goals that are unrealistic

_____ 3. Expecting things to get better right away

_____ 4. Having other people see danger signs that I do not see

_____ 5. Having feelings I do not talk about

_____ 6. Being dishonest with myself and others

_____ 7. Getting angry and upset easily

_____ 8. Complaining frequently and being irritable

_____ 9. Feeling self-pity

_____ 10. Feeling that I am no good

_____ 11. Feeling hopeless and lonely

_____ 12. Avoiding people who are trying to quit using or who do not use

_____ 13. Acting one way and feeling another

_____ 14. Not participating in shared agenda time in RY

_____ 15. Going places where people are using alcohol, tobacco, or other drugs

_____ 16. Talking about or remembering the "good old" partying days

_____ 17. Being in a crisis almost all the time

_____ 18. Having an "I don't care" attitude

_____ 19. Always thinking about smoking or using alcohol or other drugs

_____ 20. Talking about problems being bigger than they are

Others:

_____ 21. _____

_____ 22. _____

_____ 23. _____

_____ 24. _____

_____ 25. _____

Sample Using Personal Control Strategies for Drug-Use Control

(Maintaining No Use or Decreasing Use)

1. **Evaluate and explain** my progress (or lack of progress) toward maintaining no drug use:

   I think about my drug use a lot more now, and I'm using less.
   I know I don't want to get addicted to drugs.

2. **People I know:**

A. Who support my goal:	**B. Who do NOT support my goal:**
• Most of my RY class	• My friends Sue and Dave
• My favorite aunt	• The "before school" crowd
• My RY and PE teachers	• My math teacher
• My parents	• A certain person who sells drugs

3. **My symptoms of relapse:** I know I need to be extra careful when . . .

   • I hang out more and more with party friends.

   • I am discouraged and really down on myself.

   • I start thinking, "One more time is no big deal."

   • I think I can quit any time I want to, but I don't want to quit.

4. **Strategies I can use** to help me successfully cope with temptations to relapse:

   • Do a Quieting Response   • Use Snap! Zap!

   • Use STEPS   • Do healthy, fun activities

   • Get support from people who support my goal

5. **One thing our RY group could do** to support me with my goal is . . .

   • Let me share with them when I slip.

   • Help me brainstorm options for fun, safe, and drug-free activities.

   • Ask if I used STEPS when I share my decisions.

   • Call me on the weekend to encourage me and remind me of my goals.

PERSONAL CONTROL

Using Personal Control Strategies for Drug-Use Control

(Maintaining No Use or Decreasing Use)

1. **Evaluate and explain** my progress (or lack of progress) toward maintaining no drug use:

   _____

   _____

2. **People I know:**

   A. Who support my goal:
   - _____
   - _____
   - _____
   - _____

   B. Who do NOT support my goal:
   - _____
   - _____
   - _____
   - _____

3. **My symptoms of relapse:** I know I need to be extra careful when . . .
   - _____
   - _____
   - _____

4. **Strategies I can use** to help me successfully cope with temptations to relapse:
   - _____
   - _____
   - _____

5. **One thing our RY group could do** to support me with my goal is . . .

   _____

   _____

CONTRACT TO PRACTICE

Drug-Use Control

My biggest relapse challenge is . . .

_____

_____

_____

The barrier I need to overcome in order not to relapse is . . .

_____

_____

_____

The coping strategy I will use to overcome my barrier is . . .

_____

_____

_____

Note of support and encouragement from my partner:

Uncontrolled Anger Sequence

TRIGGERS

Something unpleasant
happens.

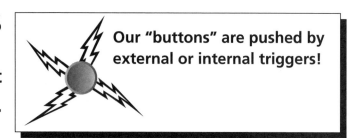

Our "buttons" are pushed by
external or internal triggers!

THOUGHTS

We evaluate.
We think to ourselves.

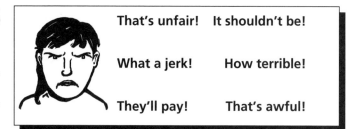

That's unfair!   It shouldn't be!

What a jerk!   How terrible!

They'll pay!   That's awful!

FEELINGS

Then we feel
the way we think.

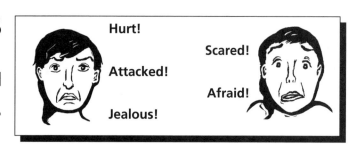

Hurt!

Scared!

Attacked!

Afraid!

Jealous!

BEHAVIORS

We act out
our feelings!

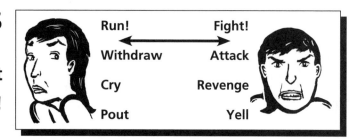

Run!   Fight!

Withdraw   Attack

Cry   Revenge

Pout   Yell

EFFECTS

Negative effects
escalate our anger!

Suspended!

Rejected!

Grounded!

Fired!

R E A C T I O N S

My Typical Anger Triggers and Troublemakers

I get angry when . . .   YES   MAYBE   NO

1. Someone lets me down.   _____   _____   _____

2. People are unfair.   _____   _____   _____

3. Something blocks my plans.   _____   _____   _____

4. Someone embarrasses me.   _____   _____   _____

5. I am delayed, held up.   _____   _____   _____

6. I have to take orders from someone.   _____   _____   _____

7. I have to work with incompetent people.   _____   _____   _____

8. I do something stupid.   _____   _____   _____

9. I do not get credit for what I have done.   _____   _____   _____

10. Someone puts me down.   _____   _____   _____

11. _____   _____   _____   _____

12. _____   _____   _____   _____

PERSONAL CONTROL

Anger Response Scores

How I Respond When I'm Angry

withdraw   ATTACK

1   2   3   4   5   6   7   8   9   10

_____

How I Respond When Someone Gets Angry at Me

withdraw   ATTACK

1   2   3   4   5   6   7   8   9   10

_____

Adapted with permission from "The Multidimensional Anger Inventory" by J. Seigel, _Journal of Personality and Social Psychology_, 51: 200. Copyright © 1986 by the American Psychological Association.

My Uncontrolled Anger Sequence Diary

Record some of the anger triggers and troublemakers that push your buttons as they occur. Also record the thoughts, feelings, behaviors, and effects that follow each trigger. Recording this information will give you a baseline to work from and could persuade you to change your anger sequence.

DATE	TIME	PLACE	TRIGGER, TROUBLEMAKER	THOUGHTS	FEELINGS	BEHAVIORS	EFFECTS
Tuesday	10:00 a.m.	Math class	Teacher puts me down	I hate him.	Angry	Walk out of class	Marked absent
Tuesday	6:30 p.m.	Home	Father yells at me.	He's a jerk.	Angry, scared	Yell back, swear	Grounded

PERSONAL CONTROL

Sample:
My Personal Anger Sequence

 TRIGGERS
- Things that tick me off
- Buttons that get pushed

Father yelling at me; mother nagging me

When someone puts me down

Teacher picking on me

Getting in trouble when it's not my fault

 THOUGHTS
- My hurtful thoughts
- My hurtful self-talk

You are totally unfair.

No one else is treated this way!

I hate you and I know you hate me.

I'll get even! You'll regret this!

 FEELINGS
- What else do I feel (besides anger)?
- Emotionally? Physically?

Out of control

Extremely frustrated

Nervous and somewhat scared

Pounding head and upset stomach

Very, very angry

4 BEHAVIORS
- What do I do? Say?
- How do I withdraw?
- How do I attack?

Get louder and maybe yell

Often swear

Threaten to never speak to you again

Threaten to get even

Become very quiet and withdraw

5 EFFECTS
- What negative things usually happen to me? Others?

Get grounded or suspended

People get angry back at me

Often feel stupid for overreacting

Need to back down, but that's hard to do

Reconnecting Youth © 2004 Solution Tree

My Personal Anger Sequence

 **TRIGGERS**

- Things that tick me off
- Buttons that get pushed

_____
_____
_____
_____

 **THOUGHTS**

- My hurtful thoughts
- My hurtful self-talk

_____
_____
_____
_____

 **FEELINGS**

- What else do I feel (besides anger)?
- Emotionally? Physically?

_____
_____
_____
_____

 **BEHAVIORS**

- What do I do? Say?
- How do I withdraw?
- How do I attack?

_____
_____
_____

 **EFFECTS**

- What negative things usually happen to me? Others?

_____
_____
_____

PERSONAL CONTROL

Sample Out-of-Control Anger and In-Control Anger

What I say to myself that spirals me OUT OF CONTROL!	What I say to myself that helps me stay IN CONTROL!
TRIGGER • I missed the bus!	**STOP** *I'll say:* Calm down! *I'll:* Do the QR. Count to 10.

HARMFUL THOUGHTS
• I'm never going to get to school.
• It doesn't matter what time I set the alarm. I never get to school on time.
• I'd never be late if I had a car!
	THINK
	I'll say: I can handle this.
	     This is not a disaster.
	     What are my options?
	I'll: Think of options. I could . . .
	     • Get the next bus.
	     • Call and see if Jeff is still at home.

HARMFUL FEELINGS • Frustrated • Angry • Disappointed • Sick to my stomach	**EVALUATE** *I'll say:* I have some good options. I can make a good choice. *I'll:* Get the next bus. If I leave to call Jeff, I might miss another bus.
HARMFUL BEHAVIOR • Swear. • Go back to bed. • Call school and pretend I am my mother: "He's sick today!"	**PERFORM** *I'll say:* If I'm lucky, I'll only be about 20 minutes late. Mr. Nye will be cool. *I'll:* Sit here and wait. Maybe I'll read that English chapter.
EFFECTS • Someone from school calls, and Mom gets the message. • I'm grounded so I miss a big party!	**SELF-PRAISE** *I'll say:* I made a great choice! *I'll:* Treat myself after school today!

Out-of-Control Anger and In-Control Anger

What I say to myself that spirals me OUT OF CONTROL!	What I say to myself that helps me stay IN CONTROL!
TRIGGER • _____ _____	**STOP** *I'll say:* _____ *I'll:* _____
HARMFUL THOUGHTS • _____ • _____ • _____ • _____	**THINK** *I'll say:* _____ _____ _____ *I'll:* _____ _____
HARMFUL FEELINGS • _____ • _____ • _____ • _____	**EVALUATE** *I'll say:* _____ _____ *I'll:* _____ _____
HARMFUL BEHAVIOR • _____ • _____ • _____ • _____	**PERFORM** *I'll say:* _____ _____ _____ _____ *I'll:* _____ _____
EFFECTS • _____ • _____	**SELF-PRAISE** *I'll say:* _____ *I'll:* _____

PERSONAL CONTROL

Applying STEPS to Anger Management

STEPS	What I will say to myself:	What I will do:
Stop	"Stay calm! Easy does it. Keep your cool."	Do the QR! Take a deep breath and count to 10!
Think	"I can handle this! Don't make the problem bigger than it is. *Catastrophizing* won't help. No harmful thoughts. This doesn't have to be a disaster. Think positively. Think options!"	Think about my options! Brainstorm. Snap! out the harmful thoughts, and Zap! in the in-control thoughts.
Evaluate	"What are my options? What is my piece of the pie? Should I cool it and walk away? Should I negotiate? Just listen? We both could be right. Which options are hurtful? Which helpful?"	Identify the helpful options. Discard the hurtful options.
Perform	"Speak slowly, respectfully! Turn down the volume on the speaker! I can do this. Use my script. I have a good plan."	Pick an option that is helpful. Implement my option quietly, respectfully, fairly.
Self-Praise	"Way to go! Nice work! I'm getting better. I got through it without losing control. I took responsibility for my piece of the pie!"	Celebrate success! Pat myself on the back!

Reconnecting Youth © 2004 Solution Tree

CONTRACT TO PRACTICE

Managing My Anger

1. A **trigger** I'm likely to experience in the next 24 hours is . . .

_____

_____

_____

2. My **out-of-control response** to this trigger is usually to . . .

_____

_____

_____

3. My **in-control response** to this trigger will be to . . .

_____

_____

_____

Practice your in-control response to the trigger with your partner. Be prepared to share how the practice went with the group.

Insights on Anger

 Upsetting feelings (depression, anger, worry, helplessness) are caused by our upsetting ideas and thoughts.

 We stay angry, depressed, and stressed because we keep telling ourselves upsetting ideas over and over (what is awful, what should not be, what is terrible). We can make ourselves more angry or depressed because we also tend to exaggerate the upsetting ideas with each telling.

 We can stay angry, depressed, anxious, and so forth if we like, or we can change the way we think—challenge our "awfuls"!

 Just knowing we need to change is not enough. Old habits remain habits when they are left alone.

 Changing takes effort, new skills, and practice, practice, practice! Remember, our existing habits came from a lot of practice, so it is going to take a lot of practice to learn new habits.

 With conscious effort and lots of practice, you will probably not become *as* upset, *as* often, or for as long as you do now.

Getting Support for Mood Management

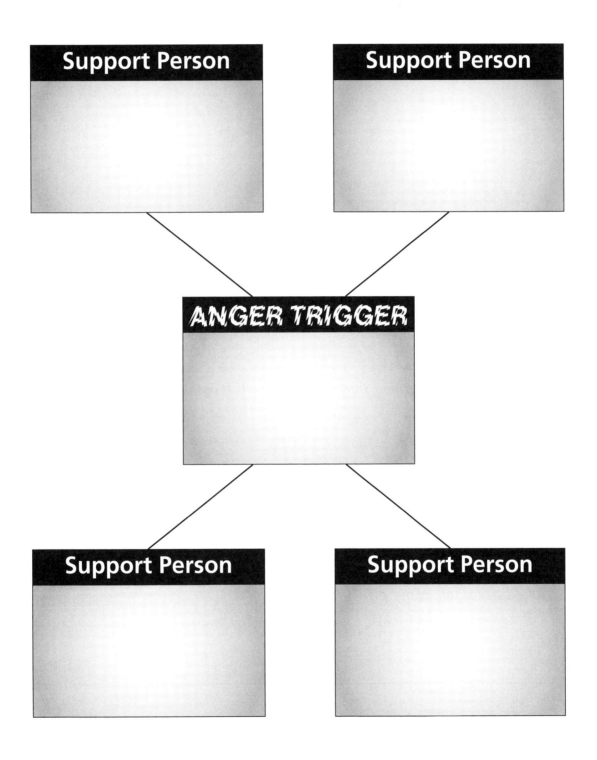

Support Person

Support Person

ANGER TRIGGER

Support Person

Support Person

PERSONAL CONTROL

CONTRACT TO PRACTICE

Using Personal Control Skills to Manage Anger

With whom would I most like to control my anger?

_____

_____

_____

What is my typical trigger for anger toward this person?

_____

_____

_____

STOP
Do a QR.

What will I do to get myself under control?

_____

_____

_____

THINK
Snap! Zap!

Stop negative thoughts. Think positively. What will I say to myself?

_____

_____

_____

(continued)

CONTRACT TO PRACTICE

EVALUATE
Find my piece
of the pie.

Determine what part I am responsible for.
Choose options. Then decide which options are:
HELPFUL: **HURTFUL:**

_____   _____

_____   _____

_____   _____

PERFORM
Get support.

Select a helpful option. Implement my option in a
respectful way. What will I do?

_____

_____

_____

SELF-PRAISE
Do a fun activity.

Praise myself for getting better at managing my
anger. Reward myself with a safe and fun activity.
What will I do?

_____

_____

_____

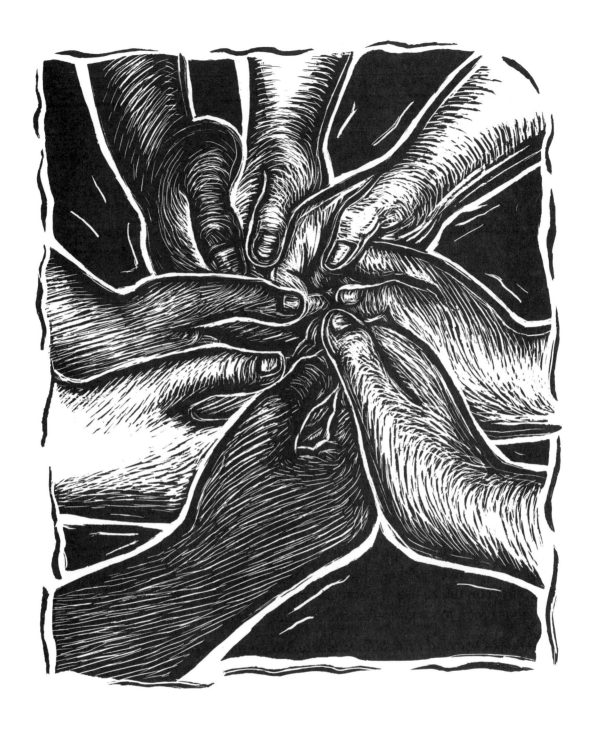

Interpersonal Communication

Batter Up!

It's a hot day, the sky's a brilliant blue, and you're ready to play. You step up to home plate, squint toward the pitcher's mound. What'll it be? Curve ball, fast ball, spit ball? You swing the bat behind your ear and focus on the person getting ready to send the ball your way.

Sound familiar? If you don't think so, think again. If you've ever talked with another person, you've stepped up to the plate of interpersonal communication—one of the most demanding ball games around.

In this game, though, the ball isn't stitched leather. It's the message. What will the person say? How will you respond? Sometimes the pitch is wild, and sometimes your swing fails to connect.

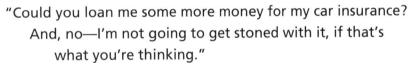

Consider these pitches. . .

"You're so much better at math than I am. I'm just stupid!"

"Could you loan me some more money for my car insurance? And, no—I'm not going to get stoned with it, if that's what you're thinking."

"I said be home by eleven, not midnight! You're asking me to believe you had a flat, got lost, ran out of gas, and stopped to help someone on the highway? Give me a break! You're grounded."

What would you say?

This part of Reconnecting Youth will help you learn how to hit more communication home runs at home and at school, with your friends and on the job. So step up to the plate, keep your eye on the ball, and get ready to practice your swing.

Interpersonal Communication: An Overview

Definition: The verbal and nonverbal exchanges between people that define their relationships to one another.

Communication Skills

1. Expressing Care and Concern

2. Actively Listening

3. Expressing Ideas and Feelings

4. Negotiating

5. Giving Positive Feedback

6. Sensitively Confronting

Good Interpersonal Communication

- ◎ Helps you **understand** and **be understood**.
- ◎ Help you earn someone's **trust** and give **support**.
- ◎ Helps you **resolve** conflicts.
- ◎ Helps you resist peer pressure with **assertiveness**.
- ◎ Brings **excitement, warmth, and fulfillment** to your relationships.

INTERPERSONAL COMMUNICATION

Four Communication Styles

We can use four basic communication styles when we interact with others—our friends, parents, family, the people at school, and so on.

1. I'm OK—You're not OK.

2. I'm not OK—You're not OK.

3. I'm not OK—You're OK.

4. I'm OK—You're OK.

Think about these four styles and look at the examples written below for each kind. Then add other examples to this list.

I'm OK—You're not OK.

I'm smart—You're dumb.

I'm nice—You're a jerk.

I'm fair—You're not fair.

_____

_____

_____

_____

_____

I'm not OK—You're OK.

I'm dumb—You're smart.

I'm a jerk—You're nice.

I'm not fair—You're fair.

_____

_____

_____

_____

_____

I'm not OK—You're not OK.

I'm dumb—You're dumb.

I'm a jerk—You're a jerk.

I'm not fair—You're not fair.

_____

_____

_____

_____

_____

I'm OK—You're OK.

I'm smart—You're smart.

I'm nice—You're nice.

I'm fair—You're fair.

_____

_____

_____

_____

_____

What Message Are We Sending?

Think about each of the four styles of communication we identified on the last worksheet. Look at the example below. Then discuss the following question with your partner: How would you describe the message that is being sent about the sender ("I") and about the receiver ("you")? Create your own examples of each of the four communication styles below.

I'm OK.   I try to be a good person, and I try to be fair to everyone.

You're OK.   I think you're probably a good person and try to be fair to everyone.

I'm OK.

You're not OK.

_____

_____

_____

_____

I'm not OK.

You're OK.

_____

_____

_____

_____

I'm not OK.

You're not OK.

_____

_____

_____

_____

I'm OK.

You're OK.

_____

_____

_____

_____

INTERPERSONAL COMMUNICATION

Communicating Acceptance of Self and Others in RY: "I'm OK—You're OK"

 1. Why would we want to use the "I'm OK—You're OK" communication style when we are together in RY?

2. Write below two examples of how we have used the "I'm OK—You're OK" communication style during the last week in RY.

- *When everyone listened while one student shared how much he had learned about handling a problem.*

- _____
  _____

- _____
  _____

3. What are three things we could do to increase our ability as a group to use "I'm OK—You're OK" more often as a communication style during our time together in RY?

- _____
  _____

- _____
  _____

- _____
  _____

Reconnecting Youth © 2004 Solution Tree

CONTRACT TO PRACTICE

Monitoring Our Communications

Think of a communication you participated in recently that was not in the "I'm OK—You're OK" style. Briefly summarize the communication and identify the communication message that it fits. Then practice making it an "I'm OK—You're OK" message.

Example 1 (student to teacher): This work is too hard for me. Besides, you're such a bad teacher that I could never learn from you.

- **Communication Style:** I'm not OK (student)—You're not OK (teacher).
- **Alternative:** This work is hard, but I know if I study and get help from you, I can get it. (I'm OK—You're OK.)

Example 2 (teacher to student): I'm really tired of your excuses. It's not my teaching. You never study.

- **Communication Style:** I'm OK (teacher)—You're not OK (student).
- **Alternative:** You sound discouraged. If we work together, I know you can get it. (I'm OK—You're OK.)

Your example of a negative statement: _____
_____

Communication Style: _____
_____

Alternative: _____
_____

CONTRACT: Monitor your communication patterns over the next 24 hours and bring to class one example where the communication style was **not** "I'm OK—You're OK." Come to class prepared to present the same information in an accepting way.

Evaluating Group Talk

Your Name_____   Date_____

For each pair of statements below, check the one that most applied to you in our last session.

_____ I spoke the way I felt.
_____ I did not speak the way I felt.

_____ I was interested in what others said.
_____ I was not interested in what others said.

_____ I appreciated comments others made to me or about me.
_____ I felt unjustly criticized.

_____ I spoke easily about the way I felt.
_____ I did not want to talk.

_____ I think I understood how others were feeling.
_____ My reaction to others sometimes made them angry.

_____ I controlled my mood and temper.
_____ I let my feelings spill out.

_____ I spoke the way I thought during this meeting.
_____ I tended to agree with what others said without adding my own thoughts.

(continued)

Reconnecting Youth © 2004 Solution Tree

If you are trying to change your behavior in group in any way, please state the change you want to make:

_____

_____

_____

Then check the statement that applies to the behavior change.

_____ I acted in this new way today.

_____ I acted the way I used to act.

Please add any other comments you wish to make about group talk today:

_____

_____

_____

INTERPERSONAL COMMUNICATION

Strength Inventory:
Strengths That Others See in Me

Your Name_____   Date_____

After writing your name on this page, pass your workbook to the person on your left. That person will think about the personal strengths you show in RY and then write them down on your sheet. We will continue to pass the workbooks to our left until everyone has an opportunity to write on each page. Everyone will be given their workbooks, and we will then share our lists with the group.

Sample Improving Communication

Directions: Think about how you might use your personal strengths to improve your communication with others. Set a goal for the next week to improve your communication with someone. Make a plan to accomplish this goal by filling in the blanks below.

My goal is to . . .

not fight so much with my mother. When we do have disagreements, I want to let her finish what she's saying before I tell my side. And when I tell my side, I want to do it without yelling or swearing.

My personal strengths are . . .

I'm kind, and I usually don't like to hurt people. Also, I'm usually a good listener. People say I give good advice and show respect for others.

Ways I will use my strengths to achieve my goal:

I'll start first by listening. By showing her enough respect to at least let her finish what she's saying, maybe we can get off to a better start. Then I will ask her if she will let me tell my side and finish before she speaks. I think if I keep my voice calm, don't yell, don't interrupt, and don't swear, maybe we can have a reasonable conversation even if we disagree.

I know I have achieved my goal when . . .

We have a disagreement but I don't yell, swear, interrupt, or walk away. When I can disagree in a respectful way with my mother, I know I'll get an A+ in meeting my goal!

Practice meeting your goal with a partner.

From *Reaching Out: Interpersonal Effectiveness and Self-Actualization* (7th ed.) by David W. Johnson (2000). Boston, MA: Allyn and Bacon. Copyright © 1997 by Pearson Education. Adapted by permission of the publisher.

INTERPERSONAL COMMUNICATION

CONTRACT TO PRACTICE

Improving Communication

Directions: Think about how you might use your personal strengths to improve your communication with others. Set a goal for the next week to improve your communication with someone. Make a plan to accomplish this goal by filling in the blanks below.

My goal is to . . .

_____
_____
_____

My personal strengths are . . .

_____
_____
_____

Ways I will use my strengths to achieve my goal:

_____
_____
_____

I know I have achieved my goal when . . .

_____
_____
_____

Practice meeting your goal with a partner.

From *Reaching Out: Interpersonal Effectiveness and Self-Actualization* (7th ed.) by David W. Johnson (2000). Boston, MA: Allyn and Bacon. Copyright © 1997 by Pearson Education. Adapted by permission of the publisher.

A Communication Model

The message = what someone is trying to say.

The sender = the person who sends the message.

The receiver = the person who receives the message.

Just as a ball can be dropped when it is thrown around the circle, a message can be dropped or lost in communication. Brainstorm ideas for sending and receiving clear messages.

Sending Clear Messages

◉ Think about what you are saying.

◉ Speak clearly.

◉ _____

◉ _____

◉ _____

◉ _____

◉ _____

Receiving Clear Messages

◉ Listen carefully to what is being said.

◉ Ask questions if you do not understand.

◉ _____

◉ _____

◉ _____

◉ _____

◉ _____

INTERPERSONAL COMMUNICATION

"You" and "I" Messages

When you are in a conflict situation, you will feel strong emotions like frustration, fear, and anger. Your first response may be to send the person a "you" message. "You" messages begin with the word "you" and focus on the person you are sending the message to. Here is an example of a "you" message in a conflict situation:

"**You** never let me stay out late!"

"I" messages begin with the word "I" and focus on how the situation affects you personally. Here is an example of an "I" message in the same conflict:

"**I** feel like you don't trust me when **I'm** not allowed to stay out late."

"You" messages tend to make the receiver defensive and more upset. When you send a "you" message, you can sound like you are blaming the other person for the problem. Sending an "I" message instead will help you resolve the conflict because it helps the other person understand your side of the problem.

Directions: For each of the possible conflict situations below, write a "you" and an "I" message that the person with the strong feelings in the situation might send.

1. A father is upset because his teenage daughter has come home after her curfew again. The father could say . . .

   "You" Message

   _____

   _____

   "I" Message

   _____

   _____

2. A child is upset because his older brother will not share a family video game with him. The child could say . . .

   "You" Message

   _____

   _____

   "I" Message

   _____

   _____

(continued)

3. A mother is upset because her son sat down to watch TV before doing his chores. The mother could say . . .

   "You" Message

   _____

   _____

   "I" Message

   _____

   _____

4. Sharon promises to return the book she borrowed from Helen, but even after a friendly reminder, she forgets. Helen could say . . .

   "You" Message

   _____

   _____

   "I" Message

   _____

   _____

5. Mike arranges to meet his friend Juan after work. Mike shows up 45 minutes late and offers no apology or excuse. Juan could say . . .

   "You" Message

   _____

   _____

   "I" Message

   _____

   _____

INTERPERSONAL COMMUNICATION

Sample Sending "I" Messages

Person 1: *Think about someone you know with whom you would like to improve your communication (for example, a parent, a friend, a teacher).*

The Problem: I need to ask my math teacher for some help after school.

What I Said: I'm afraid I've gotten lost in math. I think I've been visiting too much with my friends. Could I meet with you after school today to go over the assignment?

Person 2: *Respond briefly to the "I" message in a supportive manner.*

Yes, I'm willing to meet with you, but I can't today. How about tomorrow? And I would appreciate it if you did less visiting with your friends. I think that would help your grade.

Person 3: *What did you like about what was said? If appropriate, offer a suggestion for improving the communication.*

Both the student and the teacher gave "I" messages. It was good that the student accepted responsibility for her actions. It was also good that the teacher offered an alternative date.

Student Evaluation Request Form

Dear _____,

You have me, _____, in your _____ period class. I also have Reconnecting Youth with _____, in which we are setting goals for improving grades. It would be most helpful to know how I am doing now. If possible, please fill out this evaluation form and return to _____ _____ _____ mailbox by _____. Many thanks for your time and effort!

Sincerely,

_____

Other Comments: _____

Homework

- ❏ You do all.
- ❏ You do some.
- ❏ You do very little.
- ❏ You do not do any.

Class Participation

- ❏ Beyond expectations
- ❏ As expected
- ❏ Below expectations
- ❏ Distracting to others

Attitude

- ❏ You seem to like class.
- ❏ You seem not to like class.
- ❏ I cannot tell how you are feeling.
- ❏ We do not seem to get along.
- ❏ You seem to have given up.

Tests

- ❏ Excellent
- ❏ Very Good
- ❏ Good
- ❏ Below Average
- ❏ Failing

Absences/Tardies

- ❏ Absences are not a problem.
- ❏ Absences are a problem.
- ❏ Tardies are not a problem.
- ❏ Tardies are a problem.

Approximate Grade

A+ A A- B+ B B-
C+ C C- D+ D D-

- ❏ You are not passing at this point.
- ❏ You will not be able to pass this class.

_____

_____

_____

_____

INTERPERSONAL COMMUNICATION

Active Listening Actions

Actions That Encourage Understanding

Using Body Language

- Making eye contact
- Nodding
- Leaning forward
- Saying "uh-huh"

Paraphrasing

- "I hear you saying. . . . Is that right?"
- "It seems that. . . . Is that right?"

Reflecting Feelings

- "It sounds as though you feel. . . . Is that right?"

Asking Clarifying Questions

- "Do you mean . . . ?"
- "Can you tell me more about . . . ?"

Actions That Discourage Understanding

- Talking to someone else
- Playing with something
- Spacing out
- Making a value judgment
- Changing the subject
- Talking about yourself
- Saying you are not interested

Reconnecting Youth © 2004 Solution Tree

Get the Message?

Directions: Work together with a partner to discuss and then write down the essential meanings of the messages being sent in the following examples.

Sender's Message (The Code)

Essential Meaning (Feelings)

EXAMPLE: "I don't know what is wrong. I can't figure it out. Maybe I should just quit trying."

Frustrated, discouraged, wanting to give up.

"Gee, I'm not having any fun. I can't think of anything to do."

_____

_____

"He thinks he can push me around just because he's on the wrestling team. Big deal!"

_____

_____

_____

"I'll never be good like Mary. I practice and practice, and she is still better than I am."

_____

_____

"Why do I always get sent to the office? Everybody was yelling and pushing, and she just grabbed me and sent me down there."

_____

_____

_____

"Our teachers give us too much homework. I'll never get it all done. What'll I do?"

_____

_____

"There's a bunch of guys waiting for me after school to beat me up. What am I going to do?"

_____

_____

_____

"I'm so stupid! I don't know what I would have done without your help."

_____

_____

"Don't tell my dad about this. If he finds out I got in trouble, he'll kill me."

_____

_____

"I can't get anything done in this room. It's too noisy and the kids bug me."

_____

_____

"I stayed up until midnight studying for this test. It wasn't as tough as I thought, but I'm glad it's over with."

_____

_____

INTERPERSONAL COMMUNICATION

Showing Care and Concern Through Active Listening

1. Someone I know who could benefit from some care and concern is . . .

2. Before our next class, I plan to spend some time with this person. Some of the active listening strategies I may use are . . .

   * _____

   * _____

   * _____

   * _____

3. Share with your partner who the person is and what strategies you will use.

4. Be prepared to report back to the group on how it went at our next meeting.

Typical Conflict Behaviors

Directions: The phrases listed below describe some of the ways people act in conflict situations. Think of your behavior when you have experienced differences or conflicts with others. Circle the three phrases that best describe your behavior as you see it.

 1. Go along with the wishes of others.

 2. Deny there is a disagreement.

 3. Persuade others.

 4. Seek mutual gain.

 5. Take control.

 6. Mentally withdraw.

 7. Insist on resolution.

 8. Confront opposition head-on.

 9. Dictate a solution.

 10. Change the subject.

 11. Explore options for solution.

 **12.** Retreat.

 13. Seek victory.

 14. Try to reach an agreement.

 15. Agree on goals.

INTERPERSONAL COMMUNICATION

Identifying Helpful Conflict Negotiation Skills

Think about the advantages, disadvantages, and consequences for each of the three behaviors you circled on the Typical Conflict Behaviors worksheet. Briefly summarize these below.

Behavior 1: _____
    Advantages: _____
    Disadvantages: _____
    Consequences: _____

Behavior 2: _____
    Advantages: _____
    Disadvantages: _____
    Consequences: _____

Behavior 3: _____
    Advantages: _____
    Disadvantages: _____
    Consequences: _____

HELPFUL CONFLICT NEGOTIATION BEHAVIORS

Now think about which behaviors are most likely to result in a win-win or an "I'm OK—You're OK" outcome. Which behaviors do you think will most likely result in a positive outcome for all parties in a conflict? Look at the list of typical conflict behaviors on the previous page and think about your own experiences. Then make your own list of five helpful conflict negotiation behaviors below.

    1. _____

    2. _____

    3. _____

    4. _____

    5. _____

Contract to Practice: Be prepared to share with the group at our next meeting one story of successful conflict resolution—a conflict that ended as a win-win situation. Talk with someone you know and respect, and ask him or her, "What have you done to resolve a conflict with someone successfully?"

STEPS to Conflict Negotiation

Stop

Calm down! Identify the conflict.
- Express your care and concern.
- Send "I" messages.
- Consider the other's point of view.

Think

Explore solutions.
- Look for common ground between you and the other person.
- Use active listening.
- Own your piece of the pie.

Evaluate

Evaluate solutions.
- Decide which solutions are helpful (I'm OK— You're OK") or hurtful ("I'm OK—You're not OK").
- Decide on a solution that benefits both of you.

Perform

Take action!
- Work out ways together to implement a solution.
- Evaluate how the solution is working and whether it benefits all involved.

Self-Praise

Praise! Praise! Praise!
- Congratulate each other for solving the problem.
- Commit to continued helpful communication and conflict negotiation.

INTERPERSONAL COMMUNICATION

Sample Using STEPS in Conflict Negotiation

Situation: The neighbors ask you to feed and walk their dog while they are on vacation. You have done this often, but do not want to continue doing it.

STOP *Identify the conflict.*

I tell my neighbors that I know they count on me to feed and walk their dog when they are on vacation. I say it was okay in the past, but now I have a job and lots of other pressures and can't do this anymore. The neighbors say the kennel is full and so boarding the dog isn't a possibility.

THINK *Explore solutions.*

I tell them about a young, reliable woman our family hires to feed and walk our dog when we're gone. They say they might call other neighbors or take their dog with them on vacation.

EVALUATE *Evaluate solutions.*

We discuss the young woman and how much she charges. The other neighbors have said no to this option in the past. They think more about taking their dog with them.

PERFORM *Take action.*

The neighbors decide they will take their dog with them. For future reference, they ask for the name and phone number of the young woman we have hired to take care of our dog.

SELF-PRAISE *Praise! Praise! Praise!*

We agree to continue to be good neighbors for one another. I offer to keep an eye on their house while they're gone and tell them to have a great vacation.

Role Plays for Conflict Negotiation

1. Your bedtime is 10:00 p.m. on weekdays, and it is now 10:00. Your mother comes to your room to say goodnight. You have not finished your book report, which is due tomorrow. Earlier in the evening, you were watching TV when your mother wanted you to study.

2. You get your book report back from your teacher with an F on it. You worked hard on this report and think the grade is very unfair.

3. You are watching TV with your friends. Your younger brother and his friends come into the room and are irritating you and your friends.

4. Your teacher thinks you and your friend were cheating on a test. She takes both of your papers and gives you each an F for the test.

5. You need to go to the bathroom. Your teacher says no because you have already used your bathroom privileges for the rest of the week.

6. You are grounded for a month because you broke curfew again last weekend. You really want to go to a special concert in 2 weeks.

7. The principal has sent for you because she heard that you were in the locker room when some money was stolen from a locker.

8. A neighbor asked you to cut his lawn while he was away on vacation. You forgot, and he was angry when he returned. You would like another opportunity to show that you can be responsible. (Besides, you like earning the money.)

9. Tensions are building between your friends and another group of students. If something is not done, there could be a fight between the two groups.

10. You have been the starter all year on your soccer team, but you were late for practice yesterday and the coach benched you. It was not your fault that you were late.

INTERPERSONAL COMMUNICATION

Sample Including the Other Point of View in Conflict Negotiation

Directions: Think of a conflict you are currently experiencing with a teacher. Choose a conflict that, if resolved, could help you improve your grade in his or her class. Use this worksheet to define the problem from both points of view.

Situation: I am not going to pass my English class. I really need it or I won't be considered a junior next year. I haven't done any homework since the midterm, but I have been going to class. My parents will kill me if I don't pass.

Problem	My View	The Other Point of View
What do I think is happening in this situation?	I haven't done any homework in English since the midterm. It's hard! I got behind and now I don't really know how to catch up. Even though I passed the midterm, I'm afraid to ask for help.	He thinks that I'm lazy, don't care, am not working up to my potential, and was lucky to have passed the midterm. I know he thinks that if I would just "apply" myself I could pass the class.
How do I feel about this situation?	I feel frustrated, embarrassed, and hopeless, but I still wish I could pass.	He probably feels frustrated and hopeless, too. I doubt that he feels like a bad teacher, but I would if I had a student who was failing my class.
What do I dislike about this situation?	I don't like all the homework. I don't have time to do all the reading. I hate the stuff we read. It's boring! I really dislike the idea of being in this class again next year.	Probably the fact that I don't think this stuff is important, that I don't take the discussions seriously. I think he dislikes me. I don't think he likes the idea of my being in the class next year anymore than I do!
What do I want out of this situation? (What are my interests?)	I want to pass this class without doing all the homework. I'm willing to do some of it, but I don't have time to do it all. There's too much.	He wants me to read everything, especially the old-time stuff. He might settle for two essays instead of three. I know he'll say I have to pass the final exam.

Reconnecting Youth © 2004 Solution Tree

Including the Other Point of View in Conflict Negotiation

Directions: Think of a conflict you are currently experiencing with a teacher. Choose a conflict that, if resolved, could help you improve your grade in his or her class. Use this worksheet to define the problem from both points of view.

Situation: _____
_____

Problem	My View	The Other Point of View
What do I think is happening in this situation?		
How do I feel about this situation?		
What do I dislike about this situation?		
What do I want out of this situation? (What are my interests?)		

INTERPERSONAL COMMUNICATION

Saying No Nicely and Effectively

THE GOALS OF SAYING NO

- To control what you want to do

- To keep your friends

- To stay out of trouble

- To have fun

_____

_____

_____

HOW TO SAY NO

 Look at the person.

 In your own words, calmly say, "No."
- Explain why you do not want to do what has been suggested.
- Set personal limits.
- Talk about avoiding trouble.
- Express how you feel.
- Use "I" messages.

 Suggest another activity.
- Tell the person you will do something else that does not involve getting into trouble.

 Express care and concern.
- Let the person know you are still friends.

Practice Saying No Effectively

Work in groups of three to develop three short role plays that demonstrate effective ways to say no to drugs. Take turns playing each of the three parts.

Tempter

Tempts the RY student two times.

Lets the RY student be the "star."

Lets the RY student have the final say.

RY Student

Says no firmly and kindly.

Explains why he or she is saying no.

Uses "I" messages.

Suggests other things to do.

Has the final say.

Monitor

Monitor the process. Are they doing it right?

When they are done, give praise and feedback.

✓ Was the no kind and firm?

✓ Did the RY student use "I" messages?

✓ Did the RY student explain why he or she did not want to do this?

✓ Were other activities suggested?

Think about real temptations that occur, and practice saying no. Or, if you prefer, choose one of the situations below and practice saying no.

◎ There is a party Friday night. You are the only one in your group with a car. Last week there was also a party. You agreed to drive but not drink, but you ended up drinking. This week you decided you would not go.

◎ Your friends gather before school to smoke marijuana. You have decided that the only way you can pass math is to go to math first period, which means not getting together with your friends.

◎ Your group of friends does not do drugs. When you go to a party, a number of your friends decide to try drinking—just a little—to see what it is like. You do not want to drink (or do any other drugs).

INTERPERSONAL COMMUNICATION

CONTRACT TO PRACTICE

Saying No

In the next 24 hours, think of a situation you will probably face where you will want to say no, even though that might be hard to do. Briefly describe the situation below.

Briefly describe a **situation** where you will want to say **no:**

_____

_____

_____

What will your **tempter** probably say? *(Be brief—give one or two examples.)*

_____

_____

_____

How will **you** respond? *(Remember to say no firmly and to say why you are saying no. If appropriate, suggest another activity.)*

_____

_____

_____

What will the **tempter** probably say next? *(Be brief—give one or two examples.)*

_____

_____

_____

How will **you** respond? *(This time, say no firmly. You have the final say!)*

_____

_____

_____

Optional: Work with a partner to practice saying no. Change roles. Help build your partner's confidence by giving him or her specific praise for what was done well. Help your partner increase skills by giving one or two suggestions for what your partner could say or do. Be prepared to share in our next session what happened when you said no in the real situation.

How to Use Helping STEPS

WHAT DO I DO?

S = STOP
- Calm down! Recognize warning signs.
- Show and say you care.
- Practice active listening.
- Express understanding of problem.

T = THINK
- Introduce the idea of options.
- Help person brainstorm options.

E = EVALUATE
- Help the person evaluate options as helpful versus hurtful to himself or herself and others.
- Ask clarifying questions.
- Set personal limits.

P = PERFORM
- Ask what the person will do.
- Help him or her make a plan.
- Set a date for follow-up.

S = SELF-PRAISE
- Praise problem solving.
- Support. Offer help.
- Reaffirm your friendship.

WHAT DO I SAY?

Self-talk: "Count to 10. Get a grip. I think my friend is in trouble. I need to bring up the subject."

"I'm concerned. I noticed you've been using more."

"You seem upset. Are you discouraged? Can we talk?"

"So, if I understand you correctly, you've been trying to cut back and it's not working? Is that right?"

"What if we look at some options together?"

"What have you tried already? Any other ideas?"

"I have a couple of ideas to add."

"Can we look at each option? Is it helpful or hurtful?"

"Are you saying that _____ would be bad for you?"

"I couldn't do _____ with you. It would be bad for me. But I'd be willing to help you with _____."

"Out of all the helpful options, which ones sound good to you?"

"What if we work out a plan?"

"Is it okay if I check back with you tomorrow?"

"This was good. Way to go!"

"I respect your decision."

"You've got my support. Let me know how I can help."

"I hope you'll join me in _____." (a drug-free activity)

INTERPERSONAL COMMUNICATION

Reconnecting Youth © 2004 Solution Tree

Sample Using Helping STEPS With a Friend

WHAT TO DO, WHAT TO SAY

Situation: Your best friend has been using more marijuana lately, both at school and at parties. He's even asked you for a loan so he can pay his car insurance. Even though you thought you shouldn't, you gave him the money and later found out he used it to buy drugs. He has just asked you for a second loan to make "another payment" on his car insurance.

STOP!   **Calm down. Get ready to help! Think of what to do and say.**

Show care and concern: "You know I really care about you. I'm sorry you don't have money for the payment."

Share observations of warning signs: "I'm also worried about you. I've noticed you've been smoking more dope at school, and I think you're spending all your money on drugs. That makes me worry about you."

Practice active listening: Your friend says, "Yeah, I know. I did do that. I'm sorry, but I'm a lot better now. I've been smoking less, but it's hard to quit! I just need enough money to make this payment, honestly. Can you help me out, please? I promise not to buy drugs!"

Express understanding of the problem: "Let's see if I understand. You were smoking more, but now you're cutting back, but having trouble with quitting? And you admit that you spent the other money on drugs but say you won't this time, right?" (He says, "Right!") "You know, I just can't loan you more money until you pay me back what you already owe me. I wonder if there are other options?"

THINK!   **Help my friend think through alternative solutions.**

Introduction: "I'd be willing to help you explore other ideas, if you're willing. (He says, "Sure, okay.")

"Are you willing to start by exploring options that would help you decrease your drug use?"

(continued)

Help explore: Your friend agrees. So you introduce him to brainstorming options. You find out what he has already tried and toss in options for him to consider when he asks. He repeats, though, that if you would just loan him money for one more insurance payment, it would help him get to his counselor. You simply record the idea along with the others you have agreed to write down. Now you evaluate.

EVALUATE   Help my friend evaluate the options.

Introduce helpful versus hurtful options: "In RY we learned to choose from the options by first deciding if they would be helpful or hurtful. You go through the options this way . . ."

"What do you think about the option of seeing your counselor for help with cutting back?" (Your friend says, "Helpful! But I need my car, so if you'll just float me a loan, I can make that payment.")

Set personal limits: "No more loans. That would be hurtful to me. But I will give you a ride if you need one."

PERFORM!   Help my friend take action.

Clarify friend's choice of action: "Which of the helpful options are you going to try first?"

Help make a plan: "How about if you decide next on a plan? Tell me when you'll start."

Check-back time: "Would you call me right afterwards and let me know how it went?"

SELF-PRAISE!   Support and praise my friend.

Praise: "I really respect how hard you worked on this and the decision you've made to get help!"

Offer support and help you can give: "You've got my support! I'm also willing to help you catch up on your homework this weekend. We could go to a movie instead of partying so you're not tempted to use."

Reaffirm your friendship: "You're my best friend, and I'm supporting you all the way!"

INTERPERSONAL COMMUNICATION

CONTRACT TO PRACTICE

Using Helping STEPS to Help a Friend

WHAT WILL I DO AND SAY?

STOP   Calm down! I think my friend needs help. Am I ready to help?

What are the warning signs? _____

_____

How will I say I care and am concerned? _____

_____

How will I practice active listening? _____

_____

How will I express understanding of the problem? _____

_____

THINK   How will I help my friend think through alternative solutions?

How will I introduce the idea of options? _____

_____

How will I help explore options and solutions? _____

_____

EVALUATE   How will I help my friend evaluate the options?

How will I introduce helpful versus hurtful options? _____

_____

How will I ask clarifying questions? _____

_____

How will I set personal limits? _____

_____

(continued)

CONTRACT TO PRACTICE

Using Helping STEPS to Help a Friend (page 2)

PERFORM   How will I help my friend take action?

How will I ask what he or she will do? _____
_____

How will I help make a plan?_____
_____

How will I set a check-back time? _____
_____

SELF-PRAISE   How will I support and praise my friend?

What kind of support or help will I offer? _____
_____

What will I praise? _____
_____

How will I reaffirm our friendship? _____
_____

I'll meet with _____

on _____/_____/_____ (date) at _____ (time)

to see if I can help by . . . _____
_____
_____

Building Friendships

Directions: The friendship pyramid is one way to think about who your friends are and what changes you would like to make in your friendships. In the pyramid on Worksheet 186, write the names of people you know in the categories described below. Then answer the questions about changes you may want to make in friendships on Worksheet 187.

Interesting People: People you have not met, but who look like they would be interesting to know.

Acquaintances: People you have met briefly and know well enough to say "hi" to. They may be friends of friends.

Close friends: Good buddies you like to do things with.

Intimates: Friends who know you better than anyone. You would trust these friends with your innermost feelings.

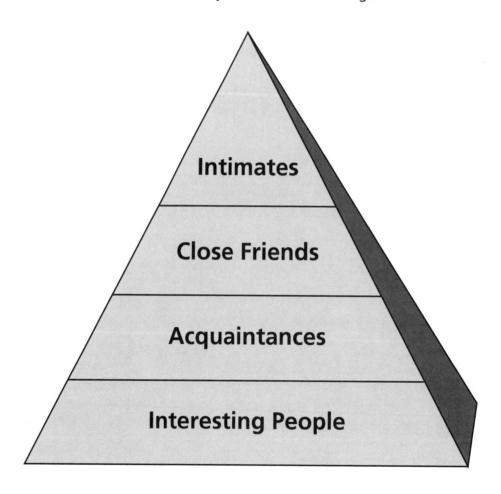

The pyramid shows that most people have noticed or met many interesting people and acquaintances, but have few intimate friends.

Building Friendships

Write the names of people you know in each category described below.

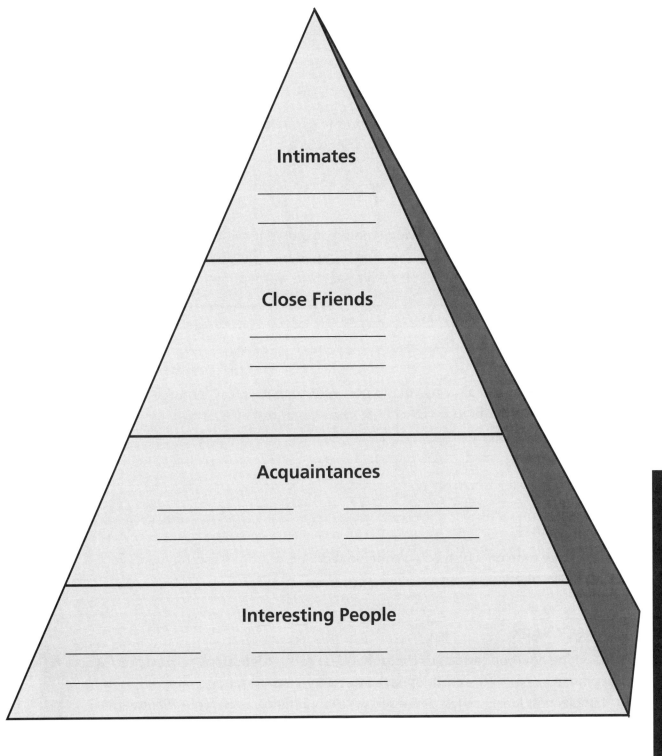

Intimates

_____

_____

Close Friends

_____

_____

_____

Acquaintances

_____   _____

_____   _____

Interesting People

_____   _____   _____

_____   _____   _____

INTERPERSONAL COMMUNICATION

CONTRACT TO PRACTICE

Friendship Goals

Look at your pyramid of friends and decide what changes you might make by completing the following:

CHANGES?

Would you like to move any people on the pyramid? For example, from acquaintance to close friend or close friend to acquaintance?

❏ YES   ❏ NO

If "Yes," draw an arrow showing where you would move the person on your pyramid. In the space below, describe things you might do to make this change. Think about the communication skills you have learned that might help you.

_____

_____

_____

If "No," please explain why you do not want to make any changes in your friendships at this time.

_____

_____

_____

START DATE

Write the date on which you will begin working on the friendship goals you have described: _____

CHECK BACK

Describe how your efforts to make changes in your friendships have worked. Also comment on how the changes have affected your daily mood. Have you been happier, less lonely, or less depressed since working to change your friendships?

Masks

Don't be fooled by the face I wear, for I wear a thousand masks,
And none of them are me.
Don't be fooled, for God's sake don't be fooled.

I give you the impression that I'm secure, that confidence is my name and coolness is my game,
And that I need no one. But don't believe me.

Beneath dwells the real me in confusion, in aloneness, in fear.
That's why I create a mask to hide behind, to shield me from the glance that knows,
But such a glance is precisely my salvation.

That is, if it's followed by acceptance, if it's followed by love.
It's the only thing that can liberate me from my own self-built prison walls.
I'm afraid that deep down I'm nothing and that I'm just no good.
And that you will reject me.

And so begins the parade of masks. I idly chatter to you.
I tell you everything that's really nothing and
Nothing of what's everything, of what's crying within me.

Please listen carefully and try to hear what I'm NOT saying.
I'd really like to be genuine and spontaneous, and ME.
But you've got to help me. You've got to hold out your hand.

Each time you're kind and gentle, and encouraging,
Each time you try to understand because you really care,
My heart begins to grow wings, feeble wings, but wings.

With your sensitivity and sympathy, and your power of understanding,
You alone can release me from my shallow world of uncertainty.
It will not be easy for you. The nearer you approach me,
The blinder I may strike back.
But I'm told that Love is stronger than strong walls,
And in this lies my only hope.

Please try to beat down these walls with firm hands,
But gentle hands, for a child is very sensitive.

Who am I, you may wonder.
I am every man you meet, and also every woman that you meet, and I am YOU, also.

—Charles C. Finn

Adapted from the poem "Please Hear What I Am Not Saying," www.poetrybycharlescfinn.com.

INTERPERSONAL COMMUNICATION

Using STEPS in Conflict Negotiation

Work together with a partner to develop two role plays of successful conflict resolution that use STEPS. Choose your role plays from the "Role Plays for Conflict Negotiation" on Worksheet 190 or develop your own role plays. Be prepared to share your role plays with the group.

STOP *Identify the conflict.*
Express care and concern, and send "I" messages.

THINK *Explore solutions.*
Look for common ground between you and the other person. Use active listening.

EVALUATE *Evaluate solutions.*
Decide on a solution that benefits both of you. Communicate "I'm OK—You're OK."

PERFORM *Take action.*
Work out ways to implement the solution. Evaluate how the solution is working.

SELF-PRAISE *Praise! Praise! Praise!*
Congratulate yourselves. Commit to continued helpful communication.

Reconnecting Youth © 2004 Solution Tree

Role Plays for Conflict Negotiation

1. You would like to borrow your sister's sweater to wear to school, but you are not sure she will let you.

2. Your mother has just asked you to babysit your younger brother for a few minutes, but you had plans to meet a friend and you are already late.

3. You received an F on a test you just took even though you really studied and tried to do well. You feel the grade is not a fair one.

4. The vice-principal has sent for you because there is a rumor that you have been smoking on campus. You are about to go into his office and face him.

5. Lately there has been too much garbage in the cafeteria. When you are going out the door, the principal stops you and asks you to go back and pick up some waste paper, which she thinks she saw you leave.

6. You are a freshman who may be late to class if you do not hurry. You have to go to the bathroom. When you get to the only nearby bathroom, it is filled with seniors who say they will not let you in.

7. You have just arrived at the library, where the rest of your class has been for the past 10 minutes. When you ask a friend for the assignment, the librarian tells you to be quiet.

8. You are very involved in the last 10 minutes of your favorite show on TV when your mother asks you to set the table. She wants you to set it now because dinner will be ready in 10 minutes.

9. Your bedtime is 10:00 P.M. on weekdays, and it is exactly 10:00. You would like to stay up until 10:30 to watch a program on TV.

10. You are walking down the hall at school, dragging your foot and leaving a long black scuff mark. Another student sees you and tells you to knock it off.

11. You have a newspaper route. After you deliver the papers, a woman calls you to complain that she did not get her paper.

Booster:
Breaking the Ice

RELAX

❋ Give yourself an affirmation: "I'm a likeable person."

TAKE THE FIRST STEP

❋ Make contact. Go up to the person.

BREAK THE ICE

❋ Introduce yourself: "Hi, I'm John."

❋ Ask a question: "Do you work here?"

❋ Make a joke.

❋ Share a common interest: "Hey, I like that album, too."

❋ Compliment the person: "Great jacket!"

SUGGEST SOMETHING TO DO

❋ "I'm going to a movie. Would you like to come?"

(continued)

Permission has been granted from the Seattle-King County Department of Public Health, King County Division of Alcoholism and Substance Abuse Services (KCDASAS) for reproduction of this interpersonal communication booster. This excerpt is from the Recovery Assistance Program, KCDASAS (1989), Seattle, Washington, prepared by Thomas D. Curtis, consultant, under the supervision of Mark Wirschem, KCDASAS youth treatment coordinator.

STEPS FOR MAKING NEW FRIENDS

Review the tips for breaking the ice on the previous page. Work together with a partner to decide which tips are most important to the two of you. Write these tips below and add other steps you think people should take to make new friends.

❄ _____

❄ _____

❄ _____

❄ _____

❄ _____

❄ _____

❄ _____

❄ _____

❄ _____

❄ _____

❄ _____

INTERPERSONAL COMMUNICATION

Making Peace With Parents

Try to understand your parents' position.

The average child in America costs a middle-class family at least $250,000 before he or she reaches the age of 18. Your parents have invested far more than money in you. They have also invested a lot of time, effort, and care—from dirty diapers and doctor bills to worries over your friends and how you are doing in school. Is it any wonder that they have a sense of ownership?

Parents need to feel that they can influence you.

Learn to live with that. You will want to influence your kids, too. Parents believe:

- If they lose control over you, they will lose you.

- If they lose control, it may be a sign that they are not good parents.

- If they lose control, you may become spoiled, selfish, or inconsiderate.

When parents need to vent their anger, let them talk.

Do not throw gasoline on a fire. Avoid getting angry back. Try to stay calm. Be willing to apologize. Admit your mistakes, and parents will respect you more in the long run.

Try to deal with conflict at the right time.

Communicate when good communication is most likely to occur. The best time to deal with bad times is during good times.

It's not only what you say, but how you say it.

Parents do not react well to sarcasm, rolling eyeballs, slamming doors, and so on. Your whole body communicates things to your parents. What is it saying? How would you feel about a dog that you had raised from a puppy if it started to growl at you? Or ran away when you called? Or hid from you? Remember that your appearance and behavior are communicating all the time.

(continued)

Avoid swearing.

Swearing is likely to trigger your parents' anger. They may think they have raised a child who has a filthy mouth and a bad attitude.

Take an interest in your parents.

Ask them questions. Ask them to do something with you. Ask yourself this question: "If I am nice to my parents, are they suspicious of me?" If the answer is yes, then you have parents who may doubt that you love and appreciate them. How should you treat your parents? People do not trust each other when they are suspicious. When we are suspicious, we look for the negative.

Change takes time.

If you decide to change your behavior and attitude around your house, give it time (2 months to a year). People are suspicious of change. **You will be tested.** You will need to show that your effort to change is sincere and long-lasting.

Although it is common to have conflicts with parents, the communication skills you know will work just as well with them as they do with your friends and teachers. You should also realize, however, that what you do may not work in some situations no matter how hard you try. When this happens, you need to practice your stress-relieving skills, including asking others for support.

Adapted with permission from part of an Interpersonal Communication unit taught by Bill Eyman in his speech class at Newport High School, Newport, Washington.

INTERPERSONAL COMMUNICATION

My RY Yearbook

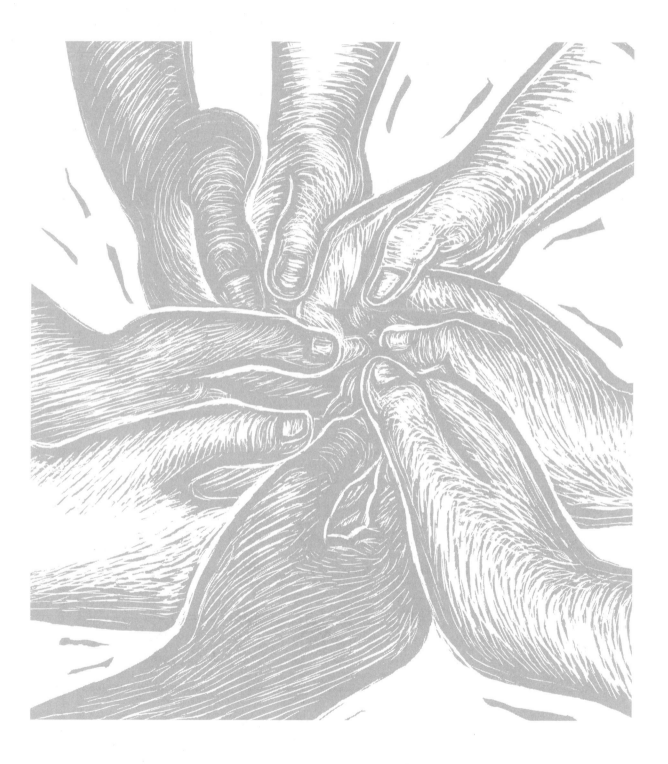